ENCOUNTERS with GOD

TRANSFORMING YOUR BIBLE STUDY

BLACKABY

HENRY, MELVIN AND NORMAN

THOMAS NELSON
Since 1798

NASHVILLE DALLAS MEXICO CITY RIO DE JANEIRO BEIJING

T0371341

Encounters with God: Transforming Your Bible Study
© 2007 by Henry T. Blackaby, Melvin D. Blackaby, and
Norman C. Blackaby

Published in Nashville, Tennessee, by Thomas Nelson. Thomas Nelson is an
imprint of Thomas Nelson, Inc.

Thomas Nelson, Inc. titles may be purchased in bulk for educational,
business, fund-raising, or sales promotional use. For information, please
e-mail SpecialMarkets@ThomasNelson.com.

Published in association with the literary agency of Wolgemuth & Associates,
Inc.

ISBN 10: 1-4185-2804-8
ISBN 13: 978-1-4185-2804-1

Printed in the United States of America

07 08 09 10 11 12 13 14 15—9 8 7 6 5 4 3 2 1

TABLE OF CONTENTS

❦

FOREWORD

‿‿

By Henry Blackaby

or me time in God's Word has *always* been an "encounter with God"! I have found that in these moments I meet with the Author of the Bible. And in these same moments I experience the Holy Spirit teaching and guiding me into "all truth" (John 14:26; 16:13–15). As a child, I observed my father's love for God's Word and was deeply impressed by the fact that he found such delight in studying the Bible. Watching my father, I came to know from earliest memory that spending time with God in His Word must be the most important endeavor of life. And so it was that I set my heart on a course to know God more intimately too.

As I daily make time to meet with God in His Word, He alerts me to Himself and His purposes in ways that deeply affect my life. When He speaks to me through the Scriptures, I am pressed to obey the One I have come to love. My obedience always leads me into a fresh transformation of my life. In particular, I experience God transforming me "into the image of His Son" (Romans 8:28 and following).

I have discovered that the Scriptures contain more than information; they facilitate "transformation" in my life, and so I am eager to get into the Scriptures each day for fellowship with God. I have chosen to have an unhurried encounter with God in His Word, and I experience His joy in these moments before Him. Nothing in my life has been more valuable than this special time with Him.

Encounters with God: Transforming Your Bible Study is meant to provide guidance for every believer who wants to spend time with God in His Word, but who needs help in doing so. Just as I benefited from my father's walk with God, so my five children have watched me, have followed my example, and have come to know and love the God I serve. Melvin and Norman, who have put this book together, have not only earned doctoral degrees in biblical studies, but they love the Lord with all their heart. Together, we desire to help others experience God in His Word. May this book lead you into a richer, more meaningful relationship with Him.

INTRODUCTION

⚛

Blessed is the man
Who walks not in the counsel of the ungodly,
Nor stands in the path of sinners,
Nor sits in the seat of the scornful;
But his delight is in the law of the LORD,
And in His law he meditates day and night.
He shall be like a tree
Planted by the rivers of water,
That brings forth its fruit in its season,
Whose leaf also shall not wither;
And whatever he does shall prosper.

Psalm 1:1–3

*M*any books have been written on the study of God's Word, each one making a valuable contribution to the topic. In this offering, however, we focus on the unique encounter you can have with almighty God as you study His Word. Because we believe this reward of Bible study is so vital to your spiritual life and growth, we have worked faithfully to present the way to meet God in His Word in simple language that will make it clear and easily attainable by any reader. We believe that as you discover God, uncovering and understanding His truths as presented in Scripture, you can begin to respond in obedience that leads to freedom from old ways of living and thinking to new life in Christ. It is our sincere desire that all people experience the blessing of God that comes from a clear and informed understanding of His Word.

In this offering, we focus on the unique encounter you can have with almighty God as you study His Word.

We have entitled this book *Encounters with God: Transforming Your Bible Study* because there is an inherent transformation that occurs every time a person encounters God. When you pick up the Word of God with the intention of knowing and experiencing God, you will find Him ready to reveal Himself. Regular and intentional study of God's Word will inevitably change your life. It can be no other way; for in His presence, everything is refined, reoriented, renewed, and restored to His original purposes. Your life is *refined* because you see yourself as God sees you. His Word shows the reality of humanity from an eternal perspective. All the distractions in life are taken away as you look at reality from God's point of view. *Reoriented* by the plumb line of God's Word, you know God's standard and have a new direction for your life. Whereas you once stumbled through life in the darkness of your own understanding, now you clearly see God's path. You are *renewed* as you respond to what God has revealed in His Word. Obedience to God always brings one into the blessings of God and restores the relationship with Him. And in His presence, your soul finds rest. Finally, you are *restored* back to God's original purpose, an intimate relationship with Him. God wants you to live in that place, constantly growing in your relationship with Him. The Bible is the tool that God has given His children for that journey.

As you study through this book, you will find three distinct sections. The first section is entitled "Coming to God in His Word: The Invitation." We will help you understand the nature of biblical studies. You will see the uniqueness of the Bible and how you should approach it. You will learn to appreciate what God has given you and how to prepare yourself for an encounter with Him. As a result, we pray that you will find the joy of Bible study. The second section, "Receiving from God in His Word: The Communication," gives you the tools to understand what God is saying to you through His Word. This includes a strategy that will help you interpret what God is saying, as well as insights into handling different types of literature within the Bible. Our desire is that this section will become a helpful reference tool that you can utilize for many years to come. The last section is entitled "Changed by God Through His Word: The Transformation." As you study the Bible, you will be challenged to respond to what God says through His Word; for once you understand what God is saying, you cannot

> *As you study the Bible, you will be challenged to respond to what God says through His Word; for once you understand what God is saying, you cannot remain the same.*

remain the same. God does not speak for information's sake alone, but for transformation of our lives. That is a choice you will make; it is the journey you will take with God. All three of these steps are important if you want to experience God in your life.

The decision to read this book is already a statement to the Lord that you want to know Him more. You have made the choice to seek after God and meet Him in His Word. That is no small decision; in fact, it may be the most important one you will ever make. So move forward with anticipation. True Bible study is an encounter with the living God. Rest assured, He knows your heart and will respond with grace.

> *Your ears shall hear a word behind you, saying,*
> *"This is the way, walk in it,"*
> *Whenever you turn to the right hand*
> *Or whenever you turn to the left.*

Isaiah 30:21

SECTION

ONE

☙

COMING TO GOD
IN HIS WORD:

THE INVITATION

CHAPTER

1

☙

APPROACHING
THE BIBLE

*For the word of God is living and powerful, and sharper
than any two-edged sword, piercing even to the division
of soul and spirit, and of joints and marrow, and is a
discerner of the thoughts and intents of the heart. And
there is no creature hidden from His sight, but all things
are naked and open to the eyes of Him to whom we must
give account.*

Hebrews 4:12, 13

A GOD-CENTERED BOOK

The Bible, by nature, is God-centered. That means that God
intends for you to encounter Him on every page. Did you
know that God is pursuing you for Himself as you read and

study His Word? He is! So prepare to meet with God and stand in His presence. The Bible was not written just to provide information about a distant people who served God. It was given by God to help us find our way to Him through the light of His Word. Can you imagine a greater opportunity for your life than to interact with the God of the universe? Do not be afraid of the Bible or intimidated by its considerable size or weighty substance. Approach it with joy! You have been invited to have a personal meeting with God! Anticipate an encounter with Him every time you open the pages of the Bible and begin to read. Remember, this Book is not like any other book in the world. Something supernatural happens to those who handle it with a sincere desire to know God.

The writer of Hebrews said, "The word of God *is* living and powerful, and sharper than any two-edged sword, piercing even to the division of soul and spirit, and of joints and marrow, and is a discerner of the thoughts and intents of the heart" (Hebrews 4:12). Can you see the dynamic nature of the Bible? Its ability to speak deeply and intimately into the souls of men and women is why it is often referred to as the "Living Word of God." To study the Bible is to encounter God Himself as He begins to work in your life. His Spirit, who actively inspired the original human writers, is present to help you understand what the Bible teaches. And as we focus our thoughts on God, He is actively at work to reveal Himself, His purposes, and His ways. For

To study the Bible is to encounter God Himself as He begins to work in your life.

4

just as God is the center of the Bible, He wants to be the center of our lives.

GOD SPEAKS TODAY

It is important that you approach the Bible with a proper perspective. If you consider the Bible just another ancient book full of dry, historical content, you are not only sorely mistaken, but you probably won't get much out of it. If, however, you come to it with the expectation that God will speak to you through the Holy Spirit as you read, you are more likely to be listening very carefully. So what are your expectations when you open the Bible? Do you want God to speak to you? Are you ready for God to speak? Are you listening for that "still small voice" that guides you as you enter His presence?

If you are doubtful or hesitant as you approach your time in God's Word, hear what Moses told God's people in the Old Testament: "Set your hearts on all the words which I testify among you today, which you shall command your children to be careful to observe—all the words of this law. For it *is* not a futile thing for you, because it *is* your life" (Deuteronomy 32:46, 47). Or listen to this wonderful promise: "I love those who love me, and those who seek me diligently will find me" (Proverbs 8:17).

Consider, also, the promise Jesus gave to His disciples in the New Testament: "Ask, and it will be given to you; seek, and you will find; knock, and it will be opened to you. For everyone who asks receives, and he who seeks finds, and to him who knocks it will be opened" (Matthew 7:7, 8). Stop and think about what Jesus said. Do you not suppose that it is worth the effort to ask, seek, and knock? The apostle Paul took it seriously. This is what he said to a young pastor named Timothy: "From childhood you have known the Holy Scriptures, which are able to make you wise for salvation through faith which is in Christ Jesus. All Scripture *is* given by inspiration of God, and *is* profitable for doctrine, for reproof, for correction, for instruction in righteousness, that the man of God may be complete, thoroughly equipped for every good work" (2 Timothy 3:15–17). Take God at His word and begin your study with anticipation. For in your search for God, He will reveal Himself to you. To search the Scriptures with a heart to know God will bring much more to your life than you realize. For you will not only find the *knowledge of God*, but you will actually find *Him*.

As you study the Bible, remember that God also speaks to you in times of prayer, in life circumstances, and through the church. So as you read the Bible, remain in an attitude of prayer and allow the Holy Spirit to speak to you through the words you are reading. As you prayerfully study God's Word, watch to see what God does next. Ask Him to interpret for you what you see and hear. Finally, stay connected to the people of God. There is a corporate dimension to your walk with God that is a key component to knowing and doing the will of God. The study of God's Word, prayer, life circumstances, and your relationship to God's people are all important when it comes to knowing God in His fullness.

As God guides you to understand truth, write it down, meditate on it, and adjust your life to what you have heard. When you get up from your time of study, look to see how His

Word applies to your life as you go through the day. He does not reveal truth randomly; everything has a purpose. What God says to you in the Bible is because He knows what is coming in the days ahead; He prepares you to live life from His perspective. If you ever get confused, run to God's Word and ask Him to bring clarity to your situation. Remain in His presence and seek Him with all your heart, and He will bring light to your life.

AN INSPIRED BOOK

Perhaps it is appropriate at this point to give a threefold definition of the "inspiration of Scripture." You will hear more about the nature of Scripture later in this book, but this will alert you to the dynamic interaction that is in process while you read the Scriptures.

> *Revelation:* This is the act God uses to communicate Himself and His will to people (Amos 3:7; Micah 4:2; Hebrews 1:1, 2).

> *Inspiration:* This is the influence of the Holy Spirit upon the minds of men, which rendered them agents of God for the faultless communication of that revelation (2 Timothy 3:16, 17; 2 Peter 1:21).

> *Illumination* or *Enlightenment:* This is the divine quickening of the human mind, allowing it to understand the truth that has been revealed and communicated (John 14:26; 16:13; 1 Corinthians 2:12–14).

When you pick up the Bible in order to find and understand God, you have an experience different from what you'll have with any other reading. God wants to reveal Himself to you and has chosen this sacred text as a means to do it. The Bible is an interpretation of the eternal—the tool by which we grasp that which is beyond us and with which we are not naturally familiar. That is why God *must* be involved in this special revelation.

It must be said that the Bible, though special, is not an end in itself. Indeed, it is inspired; but we do not become Christians by believing in the Bible, but by believing in Christ. Our faith is in a Person, not in a book. Jesus said to the religious leaders of His day, "You search the Scriptures, for in them you think you have eternal life; and these are they which testify of Me. But you are not willing to come to Me that you may have life" (John 5:39, 40). The Bible is a special and inspired Book that reveals the almighty God to our limited minds. As such, it is to be treasured as a gift directly from God. But never worship the gift; instead, worship the One who has given it to us.

COMMON MISCONCEPTIONS

When you understand the nature of God's Word, three common fallacies are cleared up very quickly.

First, the perception that the Bible is too difficult for the average person is removed. Neither the brilliant nor the simple can understand Scripture unaided by the Holy Spirit. But to those who earnestly seek God through His Word, the Holy Spirit is given to help all come to the knowledge of Him. In a very real way, He becomes your personal tutor in the things of God. God has revealed Himself through the Bible in such a way that all have equal access to spiritual truth. The key is not our ability to discover, but God's decision to reveal.

Second, some declare that the Bible is boring or out of touch with real-life situations. Nothing could be further from the truth. God is real and wants to be involved in your life. In fact, He knows your past, your present situation, and what future events lie before you. Nothing is more practical or more exciting than to spend time with God in His Word. He wants to show Himself to you.

Third, many people have a hard time reading the Bible because they don't know where to begin. The Bible is so big—a collection of sixty-six different books—how in the world do you know where to start? How do you know if you are on the right path? Don't worry, God has also provided help at this point. All around the world He has established churches that can help you get started. God has made us interdependent, and it is all right to ask others for help as you study the Bible. Depending on where you are in your walk with God, you may choose to meet in small group Bible studies or with individual

Don't be intimidated by the Bible. Jump into it and ask God to help you along the way.

Christians who will walk with you. At the end of this book, we will also give you some direction for different approaches you can take in your personal study of God's Word.

So don't be intimidated by the Bible. Jump into it and ask God to help you along the way. This endeavor will be the best investment of your time, yielding spiritual fruit in abundance and establishing your life upon a solid foundation. That is the promise of God for you and your family. Jesus said, "Whoever hears these sayings of Mine, and does them, I will liken him to a wise man who built his house on the rock: and the rain descended, the floods came, and the winds blew and beat on that house; and it did not fall, for it was founded on the rock. But everyone who hears these sayings of Mine, and does not do them, will be like a foolish man who built his house on the sand: and the rain descended, the floods came, and the winds blew and beat on that house; and it fell. And great was its fall" (Matthew 7:24–27).

2

☙

SIGNIFICANT PREREQUISITES

Now we have received, not the spirit of the world, but the Spirit who is from God, that we might know the things that have been freely given to us by God.
The natural man does not receive the things of the Spirit of God, for they are foolishness to him; nor can he know them, because they are spiritually discerned.

1 Corinthians 2:12, 14

THE HUMAN CONDITION

Although every person who reads the Bible will be edified, there are prerequisites for obtaining its maximum benefit. That is to say, not everyone who reads the Bible will gain the same insight or experience the same encounter with God. The reality of the human condition is that we are damaged by sin so severely that we cannot naturally know God. Oh, we may determine by human reasoning that there must be a divine creator; that this world is the result of that creator's perfectly balanced design. But we are, nevertheless, hopelessly lost when it comes to knowing Him personally.

The apostle Paul stated clearly in 1 Corinthians 2:14, "The natural man does not receive the things of the Spirit of God, for they are foolishness to him; nor can he know *them*, because they are spiritually discerned." This truth has been proven over and over again throughout human history. And the reason for this condition is sin. It is true that we are all created in the image of God (Genesis 1:27) as spiritual beings, but sin has blinded our eyes and has warped our ability to think rightly. It has turned our hearts away from the relationship with God to the pursuit of selfish desires. Paul described this damaging effect of sin in Romans 3:10–18. Among the effects of sin listed in this passage, Paul says that there is no one who is righteous; no one who understands; no one who seeks after God; all have turned away; no one who does good; nor is there any fear of God.

Never mistake your desire to know God for an innate goodness within your nature. Human nature is fallen; it is severely damaged by sin.

Some, however, will contend, "But I am seeking after God!" That may be true. However, it is not a result of your desire to seek God; rather, it is the product of God's prevenient grace. That is, previous to your desire to seek God, God did a work of grace in your heart and put that desire within you. As a man makes himself known to a woman in the attempt to woo her to himself, so God makes Himself known in your spirit with the intention of drawing you into a relationship with Himself. Your desire to seek God, your limited knowledge of God, and your effort to do what is right in His eyes result simply because God has been gracious to your life. You have received unmerited favor; you are the recipient of His love. But never mistake your desire to know God for an innate goodness within your nature. Human nature is fallen; it is severely damaged by sin. Just as the woman who is being courted by a man must respond, so you must respond to the grace of God. For without responding to Him and receiving His help, you will never understand the Bible or the relationship that is being offered.

BORN AGAIN

Once you recognize God's invitation to enter a relationship with Him, your response leads to a "born again" experience. This is a biblical phrase that Jesus used when He made the statement, "Most assuredly, I say to you, unless one is born again, he cannot see the kingdom of God" (John 3:3). Physically, you cannot grow into maturity until you have been born. Spiritually, you cannot mature and grow in the knowledge of God until you have been born into the family of God and have received the gift of His Spirit. Spiritual knowledge is spiritually discerned, and we have already seen how sin has damaged our capacity to know God. So listen to Jesus describe how a person is born of the Spirit. "For God so loved the world that He gave His only begotten Son, that whoever believes in Him should not perish but have everlasting life" (John 3:16).

"Believing" in Jesus is not merely intellectual assent, but a relationship with Jesus and a commitment to live under His lordship. It is not only knowing the truth, but incorporating the truth into your life. One who "accepts" that Jesus is Lord but chooses not to live under His lordship clearly does not "believe" in the biblical sense of the term.

Time devoted to helping you understand what happens when you truly "believe in Jesus" and are born again is time well spent. When you believe in Jesus, a spiritual transaction occurs that allows you to clearly encounter God in your spirit. Jesus said, "God *is* Spirit, and those who worship Him must worship in spirit and truth" (John 4:24). If you want to encounter God, your sin-damaged spirit must be cleansed and renewed.

> *If you want to encounter God, your sin-damaged spirit must be cleansed and renewed.*

The first step in "believing" is to hear the gospel (the Good News of salvation available in Jesus Christ) and to accept this gospel as truth. Paul said, "How then shall they call on Him in whom they have not believed? And how shall they believe in Him of whom they have not heard?" (Romans 10:14). You see, faith is not based upon what you don't know, but upon what you do know to be true in God's Word. There are some facts about Jesus that you must hear and receive as truth. To be born again, you must believe that Jesus is God's Son who came to take away the sins of the world through His death and resurrection.

The second step in the process of believing is accomplished through repentance; there is no other way. Repentance starts with acknowledging personal sin and agreeing with God about the condition of your life. That admission leads to genuine sorrow for sinning against God. You then cry out to God, asking Him to forgive your sin, cleanse your life, and empower you to live a holy life. The Bible says, "If we confess *our* sins, He is faithful and just to forgive us *our* sins and to cleanse us from all unrighteousness" (1 John 1:9). That cleansing from sin will set you free to enter a relationship with a holy and righteous God.

Whereas repentance is the second step, choosing to make Christ Lord is the third step. Once you have accepted the truth of the gospel and dealt with your sin through repentance, you must establish Christ as the Lord of your life. That is a conscious decision that only you can make. Many people accept that Jesus is God's Son, and everyone wants to get rid of their sin; but few are willing to release everything to Christ and to obey Him completely. Nevertheless, obedience is an essential part of what Jesus meant by "believing."

If you take all three of these steps of believing, then God does something in return that causes you to be born again. He gives to you the gift of His Holy Spirit, making your spirit alive and establishing a spiritual relationship with you. Peter declared, "Repent, and let every one of you be baptized in the name of Jesus Christ for the remission of sins; and you shall receive the gift of the Holy Spirit" (Acts 2:38). That promise is for everyone who "believes."

If you want to understand the Bible in all its fullness, you must be born again. Paul explains the difference that Christ makes in regard to understanding spiritual truth. "Their minds were blinded. For until this day the same veil remains unlifted in the reading of the Old Testament, because the *veil* is taken away in Christ. . . . Nevertheless when one turns to the Lord, the veil is taken away" (2 Corinthians 3:14, 16). Believing in Jesus removes the veil that has kept us from knowing God.

> *Believing in Jesus removes the veil that has kept us from knowing God.*

THE HOLY SPIRIT

Apart from God's Spirit, the brightest human mind will never understand the simplest spiritual truth. Truth is revealed through encounter, not through study alone. Truth is found in a Person, Jesus Christ. The Holy Spirit brings us to Christ and then unlocks the door to all spiritual realities.

We have already indicated the role of the Holy Spirit is essential in the process of "believing" and being "born again," but there is much more to say about His role in helping you understand the Bible. To be given the gift of the Holy Spirit is one thing; to be completely open to the Holy Spirit's teaching is another. Even as the Holy Spirit is trying to guide your life, you may grieve Him (Ephesians 4:30, 31), resist Him (Acts 7:51), or even quench His work in your life (1 Thessalonians 5:19–22).

But if you choose to be filled with the Spirit (Ephesians 5:18) and come to the Bible with an open mind and a teachable spirit, He will guide you into all truth. Jesus made an incredible statement when He said, "It is to your advantage that I go away; for if I do not go away, the Helper will not come to you; but if I depart, I will send Him to you" (John 16:7). That verse says that it is better to have the Holy Spirit within you than to have Jesus beside you. Jesus went on to say that "the Spirit of truth . . . will guide you into all truth" (John 16:13). That is the role of the Holy Spirit in your life.

If you choose to be filled with the Spirit (Ephesians 5:18) and come to the Bible with an open mind and a teachable spirit, He will guide you into all truth.

When you have the gift of the Holy Spirit, sent to your life as a Helper, resist the temptation immediately to study what others have said about the Bible. Don't neglect the gift God gave you, but allow the Holy Spirit to be your guide as you study for yourself the incredible truths in the Bible. Commentaries and other Bible study tools are very useful, but only as secondary sources. Trust that God sent the Holy Spirit for a purpose—to open your eyes to see the truth of His Word.

HUMILITY

There is another quality that is important when you approach your study of the Bible with a desire to encounter God. Consider the importance of what God has said through the prophet Isaiah: "'Heaven *is* My throne, and earth *is* My footstool. Where *is* the house that you will build Me? And where *is* the place of My rest? For all those *things* My hand has made, and all those *things* exist,' says the LORD. 'But on this *one* will I look: On *him who is* poor and of a contrite spirit, and who trembles at My word'" (Isaiah 66:1, 2). Do you want God to look upon you? Then bow your head and bend your knees: humility is the state of those to whom the Lord reveals Himself.

Humility is one of the desired qualities described in the Bible, commended by God and demonstrated by great leaders among God's people. Consider Moses, a man much honored by God: "Now the man Moses *was* very humble, more than all men who *were* on the face of the earth" (Numbers 12:3). Or consider Jesus' answer to the disciples when they were inquiring about greatness in the kingdom of heaven. On that occasion, Jesus took a child and said, "Unless you are converted and become as little children, you will by no means enter the kingdom of heaven" (Matthew 18:4). We can't move past that statement too quickly. Anytime Jesus makes an absolute statement about the conditions for entering the kingdom of heaven, we must take heed. *Humility is an absolute.* Humility recognizes God as the ultimate authority in life. The *depen-*

> *Humility recognizes God as the ultimate authority in life. The dependence and responsiveness of an obedient child is to mark our attitude toward God.*

dence and *responsiveness* of an obedient child is to mark our attitude toward God.

As you approach the Bible, simply acknowledge your ignorance of spiritual things and your need for divine help. Humbly ask God to reveal Himself to you and to prepare your life to encounter Him. You will discover the grace of our heavenly Father as He gives good gifts to His children.

READY OBEDIENCE

One last attitude that you must bring to your study of the Bible is "ready obedience." Make a conscious decision to receive anything the Holy Spirit teaches you before you read. A receptive heart will open the door for truth to come in. You should always begin with prayer, asking the Holy Spirit to guide your thoughts and impress upon your heart what is on the heart of God. Then obey immediately everything the Holy Spirit impresses upon your heart. Appropriate truth, and you will be in a position to know God more fully than you have ever known Him before.

Obey immediately everything the Holy Spirit impresses upon your heart.

You will discover that the Lord will often wait for your heart to be ready before He speaks; for if He were to speak through His Word and you did not respond in obedience, it would have been better not to have known His will at all. It is one thing to sin in ignorance, but willfully to disobey what you know God has said is another matter. You have just made a statement about His lordship in your life.

When you are in a time of silence and God does not seem to be speaking, perhaps He is being merciful. He is waiting for your heart to be right. He needs to teach you about His right to be Lord in your life before He can lead you into the greater things of the kingdom. So wait upon the Lord and make sure that you are obedient to the last thing He has said to you. God's ways are always right; His timing is always perfect. So prepare to hear from God by nurturing a heart of ready obedience.

3

☙

PRAYER AND THE WORD OF GOD

And take the helmet of salvation, and the sword of the Spirit, which is the word of God; praying always with all prayer and supplication in the Spirit.

Ephesians 6:17, 18

THE NECESSITY OF PRAYER

God intends to encounter your life through the Scriptures. That thought alone serves as a reminder that reading the Bible is a very personal undertaking. It moves beyond simply reading to obtain information or a list of rules to keep God happy. Rather, the Holy Spirit will intimately apply the Scriptures to your life. King David expressed it this way in Psalm 51:6:

"Behold, You desire truth in the inward parts, and in the hidden *part* You will make me to know wisdom." The main avenue through which the Spirit of God will apply the Bible to the deep issues of your life and put "truth in the inward parts" is through a combination of Bible study and prayer. There is often a tendency to "have Bible study" and then move into a separate prayer time; the two are treated as individual disciplines. You will find, however, that reading the Bible and time in prayer are meant to be practiced together; they are disciplines that complement and enhance each other.

Reading the Bible and time in prayer are meant to be practiced together; they are disciplines that complement and enhance each other.

As you read the Bible, the Holy Spirit reveals significant truth about God. He shows you God's ways through the study of His interaction with people. You see His character revealed through His action. As a result, you come to understand His purpose for human lives. The Scriptures also provide God's expectations for a covenant relationship with His people and show His provision for meeting those expectations. Prayer is your opportunity to interact with God and to personally apply what He has shown you as you read. A helpful way to view this relationship is to remember that these two disciplines have different, but complementary objectives. In reading the Bible, the object is to know and understand God. In prayer, the object is to appropriate and experience the relationship with God.

INTERACTING WITH THE GOD OF THE SCRIPTURES

The testimony of Scripture is that the Word of God is living and powerful (Hebrews 4:12, 13); it serves to provide understanding and guidance to those who follow its direction (Psalm 119:105); it offers life and comfort (Psalm 119:50); and it has the potential to produce enormous blessing in the life that will obey it (Luke 8:4–15). The apostle Paul charged early Christians to allow the word of Christ to dwell in them richly (Colossians 3:6), knowing that it would produce godly character in their lives. But notice the dynamic interaction between the Word and the one receiving a blessing from the Word. The people receiving the blessing have to reach out and embrace, and at times wrestle with, the truths of God to fully understand and implement them.

In order to apply the Scriptures to your life, you must move beyond a simple reading of the Bible to communicating with the God of the Bible. *This communication is prayer.*

In order to apply the Scriptures into your life, you must move beyond a simple reading of the Bible to *communicating with the God of the Bible*. This communication is prayer, and you don't always have to do it on your knees and you don't always have to be asking God for something when you pray. Instead, you may have your Bible wide open, eyes intently reading, and you may be talking with God about what you are seeing: "God, I see this truth in Your Word, but I don't know how to live it out or experience it." Reading the Bible will inevitably lead you to bring your questions to God. You will talk with Him about the truths you are discovering and grapple with the implications for your life. It is clear that the religious leaders of Jesus' day did not understand this truth. Jesus warned them, "You search the Scriptures, for in them you think you have eternal life; and these are they which testify of Me" (John 5:39). The Scriptures are not an end in themselves, but are a tool that leads us to a relationship with Christ.

PRAYING WITH YOUR EYES OPEN

Prayer has often been viewed as sitting quietly alone and making requests to God, or as something we recite publicly in religious settings. Prayer, however, is as simple as opening your heart and mind to God. For example, you may be reading through the Gospel of John when you come to John 14:27. As you read about the peace of God, your heart is moved to pause and meditate on what you have read. This is a time to *appropriate* and *experience* the Scriptures. The apostle Paul has told us that the assignment of the Holy Spirit is to help us understand the things of God (2 Corinthians 2:9–12). When the Holy Spirit makes a verse come alive in an unusual manner, stop reading long

Prayer is as simple as opening your heart and mind to God.

enough to ask God to show you why your heart "missed a beat" when you came across the word "peace." In prayer, the Holy Spirit may bring to your mind other Bible passages concerning peace such as John 16:33, Philippians 4:7, and Colossians 3:15. In prayer, the Spirit may reveal areas in your life that are causing you to be restless and anxious, thus preventing you from having the peace of God. If the Holy Spirit convicts you about things that are hindering your peace, then immediately stop and ask God to deal with your heart and allow you to experience His peace.

Stopping to pray during your Bible reading should not be seen as an interruption, but as the Holy Spirit working to reveal the deep things of God to your personal life. Remember that the goal in reading your Bible is not to "get through" a portion of the Scriptures for the day, but to allow the Scriptures to guide you into a personal encounter with God. Let's return to our example of peace found in John 14:27. Now that the Holy Spirit has stirred your heart regarding the peace of God and has made you aware of that which is robbing you of peace, continue in your Bible study. But remember to keep on the lookout for how God will make His peace evident in your life. The next portion of Scripture you read is John 15, describing how a Christian is to "abide in Christ." As you take time to pray over John 15, the Holy Spirit shows you that an abiding relationship with Christ brings peace.

Consider this analogy: You purchase an item that you have to assemble once you get it home. You spread out all of the parts and begin to read the instructions. The instructions, however, are very confusing; and what you thought would be a simple task turns out to be an all-day experience of frustration. How much better would it be if the one who designed the product and wrote the instructions simply came home with you and told you how to put the product together? The Bible at times can seem a little confusing and may not appear to match the world or situation you are facing. But through prayer you have access to the Author who loves you. He has given you His Spirit to apply the Word to every corner of your life.

PRAYING THE SCRIPTURES

The Bible is God's living word, serving to give life to your heart and to help you to know how to pray. If you are like most people, you will face times when you simply do not have the words to pray—when you struggle to express your heart to God. You are in a tough spot, and you don't know how to get yourself out. The author of Psalm 119 used these words to describe such a moment in his life: "My soul clings to the dust; revive me according to Your word" (verse 25). Praying the Scriptures can put words to your heart and help you express yourself to God when you don't seem to have the right words to convey the burdens you carry. For example, many people throughout the ages have found that praying Psalm 73 provides tremendous reassurance as they face adversity and injustice. In times of danger, praying the words of Psalm 46 can yield comfort and a reminder of God's protecting hand. Isaiah 41:10 is a marvelous promise to pray when life seems overwhelming. As you study the Bible, you will find that the Holy Spirit will take the Scriptures and turn them into personal prayers and requests from your heart to God's heart.

Pay careful attention to the prayers found in the Scriptures as you study. For example, if you are reading Ephesians, take note of 3:14's phrase that reads, "I bow my knees to the Father of our Lord Jesus Christ." In this passage, Paul is about to pray for the believers in the church at Ephesus. As you notice how he prays for the church, incorporate this into prayers for your own church.

The proper use of the Scriptures in your prayer life will free you to experience God in your relationships with one another. Pray for people using the Bible's own words. When you pray for your spouse, for example, 1 Peter 3:1–12 gives specific instructions relating to husbands and wives. Incorporating 1 Peter 3:8, 9 into your prayers can serve as a daily reminder of God's standard for your marriage and His commands concerning the way you treat your spouse. As you are led to pray for your children, consider a wonderful verse in Isaiah 54:13 where God proclaims, "All your children *shall be* taught by the LORD, and great *shall be* the peace of your children." Most parents want to be good examples for their children and to train them "in the way [they] should go." But doesn't it bring great encouragement to know that God promises to be their teacher and to grant them peace as they walk with Him? When praying for leaders or missionaries, Colossians 1:9–12 is a powerful prayer for those who manage significant responsibilities. Many Christians are burdened to pray for their pastor and church staff, but they are unsure exactly *how* to pray for them. In 1 Timothy 3:2–7, you will find a great description of the behavior and conduct God desires of a pastor. For you to pray that God would build these character traits into your pastor and other church leaders would be in accordance with God's will.

You will be blessed to know that the Psalms are filled with prayers that touch your heart and apply to life's everyday situations. Feel free to use them for yourself when you are in the midst of confusing situations. In Psalm 25, David cries out to the Lord for deliverance, forgiveness, and understanding of difficult circumstances. In Psalm 119:33–40, another writer passionately prays for help as he desires to understand and keep the Lord's law. These are just a few of many prayers that will be of great comfort to your life. So take time to read through the Psalms and learn to pray to God using His own words.

> *Without prayer, you cannot properly interpret the Word of God.*

The more you pray according to the Scriptures, the more you will come to see how intrinsically connected prayer and Bible study really are. In fact, without prayer, you cannot properly interpret the Word of God.

CHAPTER

4

⚕️

THE NATURE OF
THE BIBLE: OLD AND NEW

All Scripture is given by inspiration of God, and is profitable for doctrine, for reproof, for correction, for instruction in righteousness, that the man of God may be complete, thoroughly equipped for every good work.

2 Timothy 3:16, 17

THE WHOLE WORD OF GOD

The Bible is not one book, but a collection of many books. It is the sum total of sixty-six books and all are worth your study. Let's put it another way; if you only read the New Testament, you are not reading the Bible. If you only read the Old Testament, you are not reading the whole Word of God. The apostle Paul tells us that "all Scripture *is* given by inspiration of God." And in every part of the Bible, God is able to speak to His people. Most people would agree with that statement, but few know what to do about it.

Over the years of teaching God's Word in churches and seminary settings, we have found that some people are quickly overwhelmed when they first start to study the Bible. Unfortunately, many new Christians are given a Bible and are not told how to read it. They simply start in the Book of Genesis and keep reading until they get through the Book of Revelation. Others have limited their study of the Bible to a few familiar books of the New Testament, avoiding much of the Scriptures because they do not know how to approach them or understand their meaning. There are certainly some obstacles to overcome when reading the Bible, but we will help you with that in the chapters to come. For now, we want to make sure you understand the nature of the Bible itself.

IMPLICATIONS OF INSPIRATION

The Bible is God's Word. But a quick glance through the various books of the Bible reveals that many different people penned the text using different styles, languages, and settings. The personality of each writer comes through in the emphasis, approach, and background of the writing. As you study the New Testament, for example, it becomes easy to detect when you are reading a letter from the apostle Paul as opposed to those written by the apostle John. Because of this obvious influence of the writers, it is important to further consider the *inspiration of Scripture*. We gave a brief definition of inspiration in chapter 1, but let's consider some further implications at this point.

The word "inspiration" comes from a Greek word that literally means "God-breathed." The Bible repeatedly states that the Scriptures were not simply the thoughts of various men, but these men were instructed to speak the very words of God to the people (Deuteronomy 18:18). The prophet Jeremiah recounted his experience at his calling, "Then the LORD put forth His hand and touched my mouth, and the LORD said to me: 'Behold, I have put My words in your mouth'" (Jeremiah 1:9). Ezekiel's account of God giving him words to speak to Israel provides a remarkable picture as the prophet was instructed to eat a scroll with the words of God upon it. The prophet was directed, "'Son of man, feed your belly, and fill your stomach with this scroll that I give you.' So I ate, and it was in my mouth like honey in sweetness. Then He said to me: 'Son of man, go to the house of Israel and speak with My words to them'" (Ezekiel 3:3, 4).

The New Testament writers also viewed the Old Testament as the words of God. Following Peter and John's release from prison, Peter quoted Psalm 2:1, 2, stating that God had spoken "by the mouth of Your servant David" (Acts 4:25). The apostle Paul provided the most comprehensive statement concerning the inspiration of Scripture in his letter to Timothy, stating that "all Scripture is given by inspiration," or "God-breathed" (2 Timothy 3:16). The apostle Peter furthered the truth of inspiration, asserting that "prophecy never came by the will of man, but holy men of

God spoke *as they were moved* by the Holy Spirit" (2 Peter 2:1). The apostles not only understood the writings of the Old Testament as *God-breathed*, but recognized the influence of the Holy Spirit on their own writings to the churches. Paul wrote to the Corinthian church that his teaching was not from his own wisdom but by the authority of the Holy Spirit (1 Corinthians 2:13) and that he would come to them not of himself, but

> *The apostles not only understood the writings of the Old Testament as God-breathed, but recognized the influence of the Holy Spirit on their own writings to the churches.*

as Christ speaking through him (2 Corinthians 13:3). He was thankful that the early church did not simply receive his teachings as words of men, but as the word of God (1 Thessalonians 2:13).

The Scripture testifies that God desires to communicate to humanity. In this desire, He chose to speak through human instruments, giving them the heart and words to speak. Various theories of how God inspired the writers of the Bible have been put forth that are beyond the scope of this book. But it is clear that God worked through various people from different educational levels and backgrounds, using their unique talents to accurately convey His heart to people. Never lose sight of this significant point: God is communicating through the Bible to you today. It is from God; it is accurate; and it is trustworthy.

AUTHORITY OF THE BIBLE

Because the Bible is *God-breathed*, its meaning and instruction carry the authority of God Himself. A correct view of the inspiration of Scripture, however, has no value unless the reader submits to the life-changing words found therein. There is a tendency to read the commands of God and take them as suggestions or as options to consider. In the Western world, we tend to forget that the Bible describes God's rule as "the kingdom of God" and not as a democracy. His Word is not up for discussion as we decide what parts seem acceptable to follow. The Bible is the self-revealing Word of God that has authority over our individual lives, churches, communities, and nations. And God's people reveal their love for Him though their submission and obedience to His commands. But remember that the commands of God are "not burdensome" (1 John 5:3). As you obey the voice of God, He will give you life and blessings (Deuteronomy 30:11–20). James encouraged the early church not to simply listen to the Word of God, but to be doers and to experience the blessings of obedience: "But he who looks into the perfect law of liberty and continues *in it*, and is not a forgetful hearer but a doer of the work, this one will be blessed in what he does" (James 1:25).

> *The Bible is the self-revealing Word of God that has authority over our individual lives, churches, communities, and nations.*

ONE BIBLE: TWO TESTAMENTS

The Bible is divided unequally between the Old and New Testaments. The Old Testament encompasses the larger portion of the Scriptures; however, it plays a secondary role in the life of the Christian church. In fact, many Christians spend very little time reading the books of the Old Testament with the exception of the Psalms. Yet the Old Testament *was* the Bible used by Jesus and the apostles. And, almost without exception, the references to "Scripture" or "Scriptures" in the New Testament are to the Old Testament (John 5:39; 10:35; Acts 8:32; Galatians 3:8; 2 Timothy 3:16). The basis of preaching of the early church during its expansion throughout the Roman world was the Old Testament, albeit reinterpreted by Christ and the apostles.

Jesus used the Old Testament extensively throughout His earthly ministry. He did not dispute the inspiration or authority of the Old Testament. Instead, He affirmed the Scriptures and filled them with new meaning. He did not come "to destroy the Law or the Prophets" but to fulfill them (Matthew 5:17). The Old Testament revealed God's plan for the salvation of humanity through the life of Christ. Jesus could, therefore, stand before the people and share the truth that the Old Testament Scriptures had been fulfilled with His coming to earth (Luke 4:16–21). And it was through the example of Christ that the apostles learned how to treat the Old Testament Scriptures.

Paul used the Old Testament as the starting point for his theological instructions woven throughout his letters. A quick glance at the Book of Romans reveals Paul's use of the Old Testament concerning the effects of the fall of Adam (Romans

5:12–21), the universality of sin (Romans 3:10–20), the obedience and sufferings of Christ (Romans 15:3), and justification by faith (Romans 4:1–25). For Paul, the meaning and implications of the Old Testament became more significant once he understood its fulfillment in Christ Jesus. There was a monumental shift in Paul's interpretation and use of the Old Testament after he came to know Christ personally. In the past, he had been a Pharisee schooled in the Law and the Prophets. But following his salvation experience, he could preach the words of the Old Testament as the activity of God in the past moving forward to their consummation in Christ. The Old Testament Scriptures did not stand alone, but were to be interpreted in light of the coming of Christ.

THE OLD TESTAMENT FOR NEW TESTAMENT CHRISTIANS

Now that the Old Testament has found its fulfillment in the life of Christ, should Christians today continue to study and draw from these books? Some would argue, "Although Jesus and the early church made significant use of these writings, they did not have the collection of books we now have contained in the New Testament." Their conclusion would be that the Old Testament is not as significant as the New Testament. At this point, it is important to remember the nature of the Scriptures. The Scriptures are God's self-revelation to humanity. They reveal how God worked in the past, revealing His heart and character. They reveal God's love and faithfulness to His people, teach the importance of holiness and awe for God, present God's intimate involvement among people, help us know how to listen and respond in obedience to God, and show us a multitude of other significant truths. The accounts of how people responded to God and, in turn, the way God dealt with His people serve as examples for our individual and corporate lives. Paul challenged the early church: "Now all these things happened to them as examples, and they were written for our admonition, upon whom the ends of the age have come. Therefore let him who thinks he stands take heed lest he fall" (1 Corinthians 10:11, 12). The Old Testament was given to lead people into a deeper understanding and relationship with God. God's character does not change (Hebrews 13:8), and the self-revelation found throughout the pages of the Old Testament continues to draw people into an encounter with the living Lord. All Scripture reveals God's heart for His people.

God's character does not change (Hebrews 13:8), and the self-revelation found throughout the pages of the Old Testament continues to draw people into an encounter with the living Lord.

UNITY OF THE BIBLE

There is a unity between the Old and New Testaments because they bear witness to the same God. Each testament unfolds truths of God and the reality of the Messiah. The Holy Spirit will take all of God's Word to encounter your life in a personal way. Without the New Testament there is no conclusion to the Old Testament. The Old Testament, however, provides valuable background information and understanding that bring to light the riches of the New Testament. The writers of the New Testament make numerous references to people, events, religious ceremonies, and beliefs that can only be understood with an awareness of the Old Testament. Struggles in the early church often find their roots in the Old Testament law (Galatians 2). Much of the New Testament was written with an assumption that the reader was familiar with the activity of God recorded in the Old Testament. The two testaments, therefore, provide a chronological framework that testifies to the activity of God among His people. The first testament lays the foundation of God's heart and purposes, which the New Testament builds upon.

> *The first testament lays the foundation of God's heart and purposes, which the New Testament builds upon.*

In the chapters to come, we will outline the different parts of the Old and New Testaments, along with how to encounter God through the various styles of literature. Studying the Bible loses its intimidation when you recognize that God fashioned the Scriptures in such a way that they present a unified message of His purpose to bring salvation. And studying His Word allows the Holy Spirit to guide you to deeper encounters with God as He works out the reality of salvation in your life.

SECTION

TWO

❧

RECEIVING FROM GOD
IN HIS WORD:

THE COMMUNICATION

CHAPTER
5

൪

GET THE MESSAGE

Be diligent to present yourself approved to God, a worker who does not need to be ashamed, rightly dividing the word of truth.

2 Timothy 2:15

GOD HAS A MESSAGE FOR YOU

All reading of Scripture requires some interpretation by the reader. This is true of all literature. A statement made in writing might seem obvious to one person, but not to another. For example, what does it mean to say "I have no clothes to wear"? This may seem rather obvious, depending on who you are. Generally speaking, a woman would interpret "I have no clothes to wear" to mean "I don't have the *right* clothes and need to buy a new outfit." But a man would

41

probably interpret it to mean "All my clothes are dirty, and I need to do the laundry." The same statement, but interpreted with two different meanings. This simple illustration demonstrates the challenge of interpretation, even when considering a contemporary situation that is common to our daily experience. How much more careful we must be when interpreting text that was written many years ago, in a foreign culture, in a different language, and with various types of literature! The key to interpretation is to understand what the original author meant, not what we think he should have meant. But don't be discouraged; we are about to give you some basic guidelines that you can apply to Scripture as you endeavor to understand what God is saying to you.

Our goal is to help you read, interpret, and apply God's Word to your life. It is very important that you seek to understand what God is trying to convey to your life and not use the Scripture to justify what you want to believe. Admittedly, some of the Bible is written in a way that is very easy to understand, while other parts are much more difficult. You will need to use some tools that will help make your reading of God's Word clear.

RICHES ARE READILY AVAILABLE

The ability to handle the Word of God is invaluable. First and foremost, being able to do so opens the way for communicating truth that can change a person's life for all eternity. Whether you are a preacher or a layperson, your living out and proclaiming the Good News story found in the Bible are what lead others to God. For the counselor, the Bible is a tool that can set people free from all kinds of bondage. Our world is filled with pain and distress, and God's Word contains the answer to our deepest problems. For the evangelist, God's Word is powerful. Just telling the story of salvation engages the work of the Holy Spirit to open a lost person's eyes. For the average Christian, God's Word is the most important instruction Book for life. Nothing will enhance your ability to know God and His will more than immersing yourself in reading and understanding His Word. If the Bible truly is God's Word, revealing God's will, can you think of any greater pursuit than that of reading it and interpreting what God is saying? And if the Bible is meant to reveal truth and not to hide it, God *must* intend that you understand it.

Whether you are a preacher or a layperson, your living out and proclaiming the Good News story found in the Bible are what lead others to God.

HERMENEUTICS: HERE WE GO

The proper term for this study is what we call "hermeneutics." It is the science and art of biblical interpretation. It is a science because it has a set of rules that are organized. It is art because it involves more than rigid rules. The interpreter must be aware of the situation and emotions surrounding a text for a proper understanding of the Scripture. The word "hermeneutics" comes from the Greek word *hermeneúo*, which means "to explain or to interpret." A form of this word is used in Luke 24:27, "And beginning at Moses and all the Prophets, *He expounded* [NKJV translation] to them in all the Scriptures the things concerning Himself." In this passage, Jesus took the Scriptures and interpreted their meaning for the people around Him. That is the essence of what this book will help you to do—interpret the Scriptures so that you can understand what God is doing in, through, and around your life.

Readers face some natural blocks, however, to a spontaneous understanding of the biblical text. Below are four major reasons for the need of hermeneutic principles when studying the Bible.

1) The Historical Gap. The reader of Scripture today is removed by thousands of years from the people being studied. Times are different. You need to understand the way people acted in the time you are considering. For example, consider John 4:9: "Then the woman of Samaria said to Him, 'How is it that You, being a Jew, ask a drink from me, a Samaritan woman? For Jews have no dealings with Samaritans.'" In this verse, a historical gap is evident. For some reason, Jews did not like Samaritans, making it very unusual for Jesus to talk to a Samaritan woman. If you do not understand the animosity between the two, this encounter loses much of its significance. But knowing about what caused the break between the Jews and the Samaritans helps you more fully appreciate Jesus' actions and words.

2) The Cultural Gap. The cultural practices in ancient Israel are very different from those in North America or other parts of the world. Even today, you can travel around the world and observe radical differences between the way people in foreign lands act toward one another. These subtle differences must be recognized when interpreting the meaning of a text. If you go back to the verse we just considered in John 4:9, you can observe a significant cultural difference. Men did not normally engage in conversation with women. It may not seem strange to those in North American culture, but for Jesus to talk to the Samaritan woman was incredible. He broke the accepted customs of His day and demonstrated God's love to all people, even to women.

3) The Linguistic Gap. Most people today are reading a Bible that was not written in the original language. Any time a text is translated from one language to another, there is a gap. The Bible was originally written in Hebrew, Aramaic, and Greek. The words in the original languages don't always translate easily into English. In fact, sometimes there are no equivalent words in English for a Greek word in Scripture. That is why there are variant readings among different Bible translations. In recent years, we have even seen a gap between old English and modern English.

4) The Philosophical Gap. From culture to culture, there are different philosophies of life. The world view of the ancient Jews is much different from the views of contemporary readers from the Western world. One of the major differences when it comes to reading the Bible is a corporate mentality versus individualism. An example is seen in John 9:2, "And His disciples asked Him, saying, 'Rabbi, who sinned, this man or his parents, that he was born blind?'" This question identifies the philosophy that one person's actions impact other members of the community; one man is suffering because another has sinned. This is foreign to a mind-set of individualism, but not to those with a corporate view of the world. You must come to grips with the fact that not everyone thinks like you.

JUMPING THE GAP

Just the simple awareness of these gaps will make you sensitive to read the Bible with care. All four, however, can be overcome. First, reading large portions of Scripture will give you a familiarity with how people normally acted in biblical times. There is no substitute for a thorough reading of the Bible to give context for the particular passages you are studying. Second, remember to make use of footnotes within a study Bible. They are full of great information that explains what would go unnoticed by the average reader. Also, take advantage of the book introductions within most study Bibles. They will alert you to who wrote the book and the historical context of the time. Finally, there are many good books that help give the historical context of the Bible.

There is no substitute for a thorough reading of the Bible to give context for the particular passages you are studying.

The issue of linguistic gaps has been bridged for us by the many Bibles available today. A good translation of the

Scripture is the most valuable tool you can possess. There are three different theories of Bible translation of which you should be aware. First is the *literal* translation. This approach seeks to give the exact translation of the original language into modern language. Literal translation is used in Bibles such as the King James Version (1611), the New Revised Standard Version (1989), the Updated New American Standard Bible (1995), the New King James Version (1982), and the Holman Christian Standard Bible (1999, 2000, 2002, 2003). The second category is the *free* or *paraphrase* translation. This approach is not technically a translation, for it does not attempt to "translate" the original languages word for word, but to convey the meaning of a text. It interprets the original text and uses as many words as are necessary to communicate what the original author was trying to convey. This technique is used by the Phillips (1958, 1960, 1963, 1972), the Living Bible (1971), and the Today's English Version (1976). The last category of Bibles is what we call the *dynamic equivalent* translation. This approach is in between a literal translation and a paraphrase. It does translate accurately the original words, but is free to transfer culture-bound information into modern-day equivalent words. In particular, it converts measurements, weights, and coinage into its modern equivalent. It takes great care to use modern English and easy reading techniques. This approach is employed by the New English Bible (1970), the New International Version (1973, 1978, 1984), the New Living Translation (1996), and the New Century Version (2005).

Now that you are aware of the general issues surrounding biblical interpretation, it is time to move into some techniques for understanding the text. Remember, don't feel threatened or intimidated by the Bible. God, through the Holy Spirit, is your greatest advantage. He wants to reveal Himself to you as you study. So don't just seek information; seek Him.

6

☙

EXEGESIS: RECEIVING THE MESSAGE

Every word of God is pure;
He is a shield to those who put their trust in Him.
Do not add to His words,
Lest He rebuke you, and you be found a liar.

Proverbs 30:5, 6

CHECK YOUR BAGGAGE

The first task of interpreters is to understand the original meaning of a text. This is not as simple as it sounds, for readers will inevitably bring some baggage to their interpretation.

We come with our own experiences, cultural mind-set, and understanding of particular words. Sometimes we have already heard biblical stories and have a skewed perspective on the events being related. Other times we have heard an explanation of a biblical text through a poor sermon or Bible study and have accepted the errors as truth. The most common problem results from coming to the Bible with a predisposition for what we want to hear. People do not necessarily want to hear what God has to say, but look to validate what they already want to do. Whatever the case, we naturally bring foreign ideas into the Bible and have the tendency to miss what was originally intended for us to understand.

The tension found in the Bible is that it is a mixture of the divine and the human. It is God's Word spoken through human instruments. While it is true that God intended that we would read His word and find particular relevance today, it is also true that the human authors were communicating to a particular people of their day with relevance to them. It is very important to understand what the human authors were trying to convey as they were guided by the Holy Spirit.

That being said, a proper exegesis of the biblical text must always be guided by the overriding purpose of the Bible. Remember, it is God-centered from beginning to end. The Bible is God's revelation of Himself. He is the One speaking to His people throughout the Bible, and it is He who is speaking to us today. Yes, the Bible talks about a lot of different people, but only as they relate to God and His purposes. It is not a story of human history, but of God and His interaction with humankind. It does not tell us about a man named Abraham and his descendants, but of how God chose to establish a special people for Himself through a man named Abraham. It does not tell us about a man named Moses, but of how God delivered the people of Israel from Egypt through a man named Moses. The proper questions to ask are these: What was God doing or saying through the biblical writers? What is He doing through or saying to us today?

ACCEPTABLE PRESUPPOSITIONS

As you start this journey into the Bible, let's go ahead and admit that we cannot come to it with pure objectivity. All of us have some presuppositions that we bring to the text. Neutrality, however, is not necessarily our goal. We do not abandon our faith, but instead are guided by it. We don't come to the Bible as would a non-Christian who is prepared to dissect it as any other piece of ancient literature. Evangelical Christians approach the Bible with some very clear presuppositions that come out of our personal relationship with God. They will inherently guide the way we interpret the Scriptures. So let's spell out some of them as we begin this journey.

1. The Bible is God's revelation of Himself to humankind.
2. The Bible is a tool through which God speaks to His people today.
3. The Bible is a record of God's interaction with human history. The supernatural is, therefore, both expected and accepted.
4. The Bible contains divine truth about God that is unknowable apart from revelation. Because the Bible does not

attempt to answer all questions of human interest, a degree of mystery is acceptable.

5. The Bible requires the enlightenment of the Holy Spirit for full and accurate comprehension.

These presuppositions are derived from the witness of Scripture, as well as personal experience with the living God. They are foundational; they guide the path of interpretation. So let's now look more closely at our task as interpreters of God's Word.

EXEGESIS: YOU CAN DO IT

"Exegesis" is a term used to describe the careful study of Scripture to discover the original and intended meaning of a text. Everyone is an exegete; some are good and some are bad. You have probably heard someone say, "back in those days . . . " or "what Jesus really meant was . . ." Those sayings are an exegetical analysis of a text. The speaker is trying to overcome the gaps between an ancient text and modern understandings.

Exegesis is utilized when trying to describe why we don't greet with a "holy kiss" (1 Peter 5:14) or welcome guests into our homes by washing their feet (John 13:14). It explains why we don't literally pluck out our right eye or cut off our right hand if they cause us to sin (Matthew 5:29, 30). It interprets the shocking words of Jesus that "unless you eat the flesh of the Son of Man and drink His blood, you have no life in you" (John 6:53). Exegesis brings meaning to symbolic language that makes no sense. Consider the bizarre description of Jesus by the apostle John, and try to picture what this would literally look like: "His head and hair *were* white like wool, as white as snow, and His eyes like a flame of fire; His feet *were* like fine brass, as if refined in a furnace, and His voice as the sound of many waters; He had in His right hand seven stars, out of His mouth went a sharp two-edged sword, and His countenance *was* like the sun shining in its strength" (Revelation 1:14–16). As you can see, exegesis is needed to understand the Word of God in all its fullness.

> *"Exegesis" is a term used to describe the careful study of Scripture to discover the original and intended meaning of a text.*

WATCH YOUR STEP

There are many pitfalls, however, that poor exegetes can fall into as they mishandle the Word of God. People have a tendency to explain away anything they don't like as "culture bound" or in some way irrelevant to modern society. They can take a word in Scripture and project a contemporary meaning onto it that is inappropriate for its original use. They can take a text that is "descriptive" of a historical event and make it a "prescriptive" command for Christians to follow today. They can take a statement out of context and draw all kinds of ridiculous conclusions.

Let's consider a couple examples of poor exegesis to give you a feel for the pitfalls. Philippians 4:13 is a statement that has been greatly misused. Paul made a wonderful declaration, "I can do all things through Christ who strengthens me." Taken out of context, however, one could draw some far-fetched conclusions about what Christ will help us do. Can you claim this promise to help you be a super star athlete? Will He give you business savvy to become extremely wealthy? Or perhaps fulfill your lifelong dream to fly to the moon? "All things" must be qualified, or it becomes a license to do *anything* in the name of Christ. Obviously, Christ will not strengthen you to do something outside of His will. This verse is often used out of self-centered ambition and not out of the desire to obey Christ. Looking at the context of this verse, we see that Paul was actually talking about being content in all circumstances. Paul had known life in abundance, but he had also endured hunger and suffered through great need. Yet Christ had given him strength for all circumstances, and his relationship with Christ had brought contentment.

An improper use of word studies can also lead to conclusions that are misleading. In Romans 1:16, Paul wrote: "I am not ashamed of the gospel of Christ, for it is the power of God to salvation for everyone who believes." In this verse, the word "power" is a translation from the Greek word *dúnamis*. You can easily see it in the English word "dynamite," which has the same etymological roots. There are many preachers who have stirred up the crowds by declaring that the gospel is the "dynamite" of God for salvation. Its explosive power can transform a life in dramatic fashion. The problem, however, is that our picture of dynamite is forced back into time and put into Paul's mouth—something he had no intention of saying. Paul neither had a concept of dynamite as we now know it, nor would he have used it if he had known it. Dynamite destroys, blows things up, breaks things apart, and can even be used to take life. The gospel, however, does the opposite. Paul is expressing the fact that the gospel brings wholeness and gives new life. Which has more power: that which takes life, or that which gives life? A proper exegesis of this passage would stay true to the original intent and resist pushing a meaning beyond its natural bounds for dramatic effect.

START WALKING

The best way to master the Bible is just to start your study of it. Clearly, not everyone will be an expert in exegesis, but some helpful tools will allow anybody to dig into the Scriptures and find abundant and relevant truth. An "expert" is one who is diligent to master the biblical languages, Jewish and Hellenist backgrounds, ancient manuscript variations, and broader background information of the ancient world. But you, too, can do good exegesis even if you don't have access to such tools. You can develop your own skills and learn to utilize the results of "expert" research for your own purposes. You can be a good exegete who understands what God was saying to the original audience and discern its timeless truth for today.

The key to good exegesis is to read the Bible carefully and thoughtfully. You will need to ask some questions of yourself and the text if you want to discover what God is saying through the human authors. This process may seem rigid at first, but it will become very natural as you develop good habits in reading the Bible. The following chapters will explain this in detail.

CHAPTER

7

❧

QUESTIONS FOR PERSONAL PREPARATION

"You search the Scriptures, for in them you think you have eternal life; and these are they which testify of Me. But you are not willing to come to Me that you may have life."

John 5:39, 40

FIRST THINGS FIRST

Any time you come to the Bible with the intention of meeting with God, you need to prepare for such an encounter. If Bible study truly is an encounter with God whereby we expect Him to speak, we must ready ourselves for that moment. That is why we need to begin with asking questions for personal preparation. We encourage you to genuinely ask yourself a series of questions that are an important part of interpretation and hearing from God through the Scriptures.

Remember, the Pharisees in Jesus' day had all the right tools for biblical interpretation. That is, all but one important tool. Your relationship to God is the greatest hermeneutical key to unlocking the Scriptures. Principles of literary interpretation are inadequate by themselves, if we truly believe that God speaks to His people through the Scriptures. Rules for interpreting the Bible must be guided by a relationship to the God of the Bible. It can be no other way. If we teach people how to study the Bible without the relationship, we will produce Pharisees, not disciples. If we teach people to pray and seek the relationship without Bible study, we will produce shallow and fickle believers who will be tossed about by every wind of doctrine that may blow their way. The two must be in balance.

Rules for interpreting the Bible must be guided by a relationship to the God of the Bible. It can be no other way.

Jesus turned to the Pharisees of His day and said, "You search the Scriptures, for in them you think you have eternal life; and these are they which testify of Me. But you are not willing to come to Me that you may have life" (John 5:39, 40). We cannot stress enough how important personal preparation is in biblical interpretation. Approaching Bible study without a healthy and growing relationship to God is like trying to go to the moon without a spacecraft. One may jump three inches, another eight inches, and still another fifteen inches. But nobody will come close to reaching the moon just by jumping. Similarly, your relationship to God through Jesus Christ is the vehicle God uses to help you hear and understand His Word, the Bible; and you can't really be successful without this relationship. So as you come to the Bible, ask yourself the following questions:

Question #1: Is my heart clean before God?

When you come to the Bible with the intention of meeting with God, you need to prepare yourself for entering a holy place. The psalmist asked: "Who may ascend into the hill of the LORD? Or who may stand in His holy place? He who has clean hands and a pure heart, who has not lifted up his soul to an idol, nor sworn deceitfully. He shall receive a blessing from the LORD, and righteousness from the God of his salvation. This *is* Jacob, the generation of those who seek Him, who seek Your face" (Psalm 24:3–6). Bible study, in its purest form, is an encounter with God. You cannot walk into God's presence as you would into the presence of any other person. He is God! He will either see you washed in the blood of Christ and clothed in His righteousness, or He will see your sin. God will not open your eyes to

> *God will not open your eyes to see His kingdom until He first opens your eyes to see your sin.*

see His kingdom until He first opens your eyes to see your sin.

Cleansing must happen before He takes your hand and walks you through the Most Holy Place. David said, "Search me, O God, and know my heart; try me, and know my anxieties; and see if *there is any* wicked way in me, and lead me in the way everlasting" (Psalm 139:23, 24). Allow Him to search your heart and bring cleansing of sin, so that He may lead you in "the way everlasting." This is the first question you must ask God. You cannot skip this step in biblical interpretation, for it is the door that leads you into the Holy Place where God can show you the deeper things of the kingdom. Here is the promise for you: "If we confess our sins, He is faithful and just to forgive us *our* sins and to cleanse us from all unrighteousness" (1 John 1:9).

Question #2: Is there current evidence of the Holy Spirit in my life?

The presence of the Holy Spirit in your life is also necessary for biblical interpretation. Once you have had your sin removed through repentance, you must also be filled with the Holy Spirit. This is not just the initial work of salvation, but the continual work of the Holy Spirit in your life. Jesus said, "When He, the Spirit of truth, has come, He will guide you into all truth; for He will not speak on His own *authority*, but whatever He hears He will speak; and He will tell you things to come" (John 16:13). Wow! Can you see how important the role of the Holy Spirit is in biblical interpretation?

So the question is not "Were you saved?" You need to ask if there is current evidence of the Holy Spirit controlling your life and leading you to know and do the will of the Lord. An easy way to know this is to put your life against the plumb line of God's word in Galatians 5:22, 23. Can you see the fruit of the Spirit in your life: "love, joy, peace, longsuffering, kindness, goodness, faithfulness, gentleness, self-control"? These qualities are not determined by your circumstances, but by the Holy Spirit. If He is in control of your life, He will be producing these Christlike qualities.

> *Can you see the fruit of the Spirit in your life: "love, joy, peace, longsuffering, kindness, goodness, faithfulness, gentleness, self-control"?*

Take a moment and let the Holy Spirit search your heart and help you see your life as He sees it. Is He in control? Is He making a visible difference? Are you filled with the Spirit of God? If you do not have confidence in this area of your life, ask Him to fill you. Don't take it for granted, but keep asking Him to do in your life what you cannot do on your own. Then watch as He takes the Scriptures and guides you into all truth.

Question #3: What has God recently said to me?

God does not speak in isolation or move in some way detached from what He is already doing. He knows what He is doing and where He is going. So take a moment and review what you know God has already been speaking to you about in previous times of study. Jesus said, "The Helper, the Holy Spirit, whom the Father will send in My name, He will teach you all things, and bring to your remembrance all things that I said to you" (John 14:26). One of the assignments of the Holy Spirit is to help you remember what the Lord has said to you. That will be important, for His words will guide you to know the Father's will. Each step leads to another, building one upon another. So as you consider what God wants to say to you today, remain cognizant of what He *has been* saying. This will give you a context in which you can hear and understand.

As you consider what God wants to say to you today, remain cognizant of what He has been saying. This will give you a context in which you can hear and understand.

Take a moment and ask the Holy Spirit to bring to your mind what you have already heard from God in the Bible. Meditate for a moment as you regain your awareness of His activity in your life. Look around your life and allow the Holy Spirit to help you understand your circumstances in terms of the activity of God. Be sensitive to what God is doing so that you will be ready to respond to Him as He speaks to you through His Word.

Question #4: Am I obeying the last thing God said?

Jesus turned to those who were following Him and said, "Why do you call me 'Lord, Lord,' and not do the things which I say?" (Luke 6:46). You see, *calling* Christ "Lord" does not mean He *is* Lord of your life. We can fool ourselves into thinking that Christ will show us all things because we are Christians. That is just not true. Obedience reveals our relationship and will lead us into greater encounters with Him. If you have not done the last thing Christ said, why would He tell you something new?

As far as God is concerned, what you *do* reveals what you *believe* about Him, no matter what you say. If you have not obeyed the last thing He said, He most likely will not say anything else until you understand His lordship. So go back and see if there are things hanging in your life—things that have been left undone. Ask the Lord to help you put into practice what He has already been saying through His Word.

> *As far as God is concerned, what you do reveals what you believe about Him, no matter what you say.*

Question #5: Am I ready to respond in obedience to what God is about to say?

A heart of ready obedience is critical when it comes to hearing God speak through His Word. You must answer God before you begin your study of His Word. You may say, "How can I give an answer before I know what He said?" "If I don't know what God is saying, how can I respond?" Listen carefully: You must give your answer *before* you ever hear God speak. The only way you can know God is to accept Jesus Christ as your Lord and Savior. And if you have made the decision to make Christ Lord, then you only have one answer:

If you have made the decision to make Christ Lord, then you only have one answer: "YES, Lord."

"YES, Lord." Before you ever hear Him, you must answer "yes." A heart of ready obedience is necessary for Him to freely speak. So what is your answer? If there is a hesitation, don't expect to hear Him. You have not yet accepted the fact that He is Lord. If that question is not answered, He can't give you an assignment; He can't entrust to you the greater things of the kingdom. He will simply talk to you about His right to be Lord.

So take a moment and recognize God's right to your life and let Him know that your answer is "yes" no matter what He says. You have no idea what freedom that brings to your Bible study. When God knows you are ready to respond, He can talk to you about what is on His heart.

THE PRIVILEGE OF RELATIONSHIP

Now that you know the right questions to ask, you will be able to keep your relationship to Christ up to date. When the relationship is what it should be, you are in a position to see the Bible come alive. The Scripture says that Jesus "turned to *His* disciples and said privately, 'Blessed *are* the eyes which see the things you see; for I tell you that many prophets and kings have desired to see what you see, and have not seen *it*, and to hear what you hear, and have not heard *it*" (Luke 10:23, 24). You will discover that walking with Jesus allows you to see many more things than you ever imagined. The relationship is the goal; it is what the Christian life is all about. You must understand that Bible study is not an exercise to learn more about God. Bible study is the privilege of walking with Him. It doesn't *lead* you to an encounter with God; it *is* the encounter.

CHAPTER

8

❦

QUESTIONS FOR TEXTUAL INTERPRETATION

Yes, if you cry out for discernment,
And lift your voice for understanding,
If you seek her as silver,
And search for her as for hidden treasures;
Then you will understand the fear of the LORD,
And find the knowledge of God.

Proverbs 2:3–5

TAKE A LOOK AROUND

Nothing in the Bible should be taken in isolation. Whether you are looking at a word, a sentence, a paragraph, or a book, everything has a context. Even though we are primarily interested in what God is saying, He chose to speak through human language. That human language has meaning and is very important to understand. When approaching a text, you need to ask some necessary questions to discover its true meaning. Depending on the text, the answers to these questions are sometimes obvious and clear. Other times you may need to put forth effort and utilize further research before you fully understand the text. The following questions will help you in your study.

Whether you are looking at a word, a sentence, or a book, everything has a context.

Question #1: What do the words mean?

This question seems rather obvious, but it is still very important to ask. When answering this question, always seek the common meaning of the language first. In determining the proper meaning of the words, be aware of the following issues.

The study of "word meaning" requires more attention than one might first think, for many words have both a denotation and a connotation. The denotation of a word is its specific meaning in a dictionary. The connotation, however, is an implied emotional meaning of a word apart from its formal meaning; it is not explicitly stated. For example, to be called an *innovative pacemaker* would be a positive thing. But to be called a *grueling taskmaster* would be negative. Both descriptions could be said of the same person, but with a different emotional response. Furthermore, words and phrases can have both a technical meaning and a popular meaning. For example, *foot-in-mouth disease* means something different from just the technical meaning of each individual word.

Another consideration when it comes to the meaning of words is that they can have a range of meanings. Word studies, therefore, are a constant exercise in interpretation. First of all, words can be given a special sense in the Bible that is not found in other literature written at that time. This is true of words like "justification," "sin," "love," "baptism," and "cross." Second, words can have more than one meaning, even in the same book. The word "death" could be used to describe people who physically die, people who are dead in sins before accepting Christ, or people who die to self when they become a Christian. Third, one English word can be used to translate several different Greek words. An example of this is the word "love," which is used to translate three different Greek words. Just by looking at the English word "love," you would not be able to tell exactly what kind of love the writer is referring to in the passage.

There are six steps in discovering the meaning of a word in the Bible. Use them in this order as you seek better understanding. 1) Look at the immediate context to find the meaning. A good dictionary will help with this initial step. 2) Look at other versions of the Bible to see variant translations of the word. 3) Look at other occurrences of the word within the book itself with the help of a Bible concordance. 4) Find occurrences of the word in other writings by the same author with the use of a concordance. 5) Discover the usage of the word by other authors, also by using a concordance. 6) If you are studying a rare biblical word, you may want to use a lexicon to pursue nonbiblical usage in other literature.

Question #2: What is the literary context?

If you read other books on biblical interpretation, you will have come across the term "Lexical–Syntactical Principle." "Lexical" refers to the meanings of the words, which we have just considered. "Syntactical" is the arrangement of words to form sentences. Words only have meaning as they form sentences and develop the writer's message. It is important to broaden your view from a specific verse to the surrounding verses and larger train of thought. Many Bibles have inserted headings that identify sections of material and allow you to quickly see how the writer is grouping various thoughts. While these headings are not in the original text, they are helpful in determining how much you ought to read to encompass the immediate context.

Many Bibles have inserted headings that identify sections of material and allow you to quickly see how the writer is grouping various thoughts.

Consider the following example: Jesus said, "If anyone comes to Me and does not hate his father and mother, wife and children, brothers and sisters, yes, and his own life also, he cannot be My disciple" (Luke 14:26). Is Jesus saying that we must "hate" our family if we want to follow Him? This verse, taken out of context, could be used to draw some terrible conclusions. But when you read the larger context of Luke 14:15–35, Jesus' radical statement becomes clear. He was on the way to the cross when He turned to the multitudes and challenged them to count the cost of discipleship. His vivid description was for the purpose of comparison; love for God should not be challenged by any other devotion in life. He was not teaching on family relationships; He was stressing an important truth of discipleship. When it comes to a relationship with your parents, Jesus undergirded the fifth commandment to "honor your father and mother" (Matthew 15:6).

Remember that the Bible is written in human language and that human language can be expressed with many different styles of literature. Each passage in the Bible is written in a specific literary form. It is always best to quickly identify the style of writing, for that may dramatically change the way you will interpret the text. Several literary styles and their interpretive principles will be discussed in detail in chapters 11—18.

Question #3: What is the historical context?

The text you are studying happened in a particular place and a particular moment in time. Those facts are very relevant to understanding the meaning intended by the writer. Consider the following statement in Philippians 4:4: "Rejoice in the Lord always. Again I will say, rejoice!" If you read this while in a very difficult circumstance, you might reply, "That is easy for you to say; you don't know the trials I am going through right now." You might even have an attitude of resentment, feeling that the Bible is irrelevant and idealistic. But to understand the historical context fills this verse with meaning, making it very relevant to daily life.

This statement was made by the apostle Paul. How acquainted was he with trials? We will probably never know all that Paul endured, but he gave us a glimpse in 2 Corinthians 11:24–27: "From the Jews five times I received forty *stripes* minus one. Three times I was beaten with rods; once I was stoned; three times I was shipwrecked; a night and a day I have been in the deep; *in* journeys often, *in* perils of waters, *in* perils of robbers, *in* perils of *my own* countrymen, *in* perils of the Gentiles, *in* perils in the city, *in* perils in the wilderness, *in* perils in the sea, *in* perils among false brethren; in weariness and toil, in sleeplessness often, in hunger and thirst, in fastings often, in cold and nakedness." You think you have had a bad day? Paul understood pain and suffering. And when he said, "Rejoice in the Lord always," he meant *always* and in every circumstance. In fact, Paul wrote these words while he was in a Roman prison. His exhortation to the Christians in Philippi has a much greater impact when you know his situation. Context is important to fully appreciate a text.

In discovering the historical context, read the introduction at the beginning of a book. A good study Bible will give you information about the author, the place, the time, and the important issues of day. You may also want to consult other reference books or commentaries for further insights into the text.

Context is important to fully appreciate a text.

Question #4: What does the rest of the Bible say about this passage?

The best commentary on the Bible is the Bible itself, for it often speaks to a subject more than once. And if the Lord wants us to grasp a really significant truth, He will make sure it is discussed throughout the Scriptures. The basic principle is this: allow the clear passages to interpret the unclear or obscure passages.

> *The basic principle is this: allow the clear passages to interpret the unclear or obscure passages.*

Consider the statement in Hebrews 9:22: "Without shedding of blood there is no remission." This statement deals with the forgiveness or "remission" of sins. Does this verse teach that bloodshed is necessary every time a person asks for forgiveness? Yes and no. Yes, it does teach that there is no forgiveness of sin without the shedding of blood. But the New Testament teaches that the practice of animal sacrifice has been replaced by the one-time sacrifice of the "Lamb of God." First Peter 1:18, 19 says that "you were not redeemed with corruptible things, *like* silver or gold . . . but with the precious blood of Christ, as of a lamb without blemish and without spot." Furthermore, Hebrews 10:12, 14 teaches us that "this Man, after He had offered one sacrifice for sins forever, sat down at the right hand of God. . . . For by one offering He has perfected forever those who are being sanctified." Can you see how the Bible is its best commentator? Significant statements are understood in the light of the entire Bible.

Once you learn to use a good cross-reference tool, it will be your best friend. Many study Bibles have a center column in the text that points you to other passages that complement the text you are studying. When reading in the Gospels, utilize a "Gospel parallel" book that allows you to see the same stories or events side by side. Sometimes the variant readings can give insight or further understanding to a text. When you are dealing with significant doctrines, make sure you bring your reading in line with the major teaching on the subject in other parts of the Bible. For example: the Resurrection is thoroughly discussed in 1 Corinthians 15; faith in Hebrews 11; the effect of sin in Romans 3; the role of the Holy Spirit in John 16; love for the family of God in 1 Corinthians 13 or 1 John 4. You should never take an isolated verse and build a whole doctrine around it. Always bring your text in line with the rest of the Bible, and allow the clear passages to bring light to those that are confusing.

Question #5: What is the singular purpose of the author?

Always assume that the writer of a text had one purpose in mind when the passage was written. In discovering what the author was trying to convey, you must start with understanding the author. Who wrote the book? Why did he write the book? What situation was he addressing in the book?

Always assume that the writer of a text had one purpose in mind when the passage was written.

Look at the book you are reading and trace the development of the author's theme. Show how the present passage fits into the context of what the author has said in other parts of the book. For example, Peter wrote that the "end of all things is at hand" (1 Peter 4:7). The end of what? The theme of Peter indicates that he was talking about the return of Christ.

There is another important question to ask of the text when determining the purpose of the author. Is the author giving a description or a prescription? In other words, if the intention of the author is to give a historical record of events, do not take his description of what happened and make it a command for us to follow today. If, however, the author is giving instruction for believers to follow, then we can apply it to our lives, too. A descriptive statement is simply an observation of what happened with no obligation to reproduce it. A prescriptive statement is an account of what happened for the purpose of instruction or creating a normative pattern to follow.

When considering descriptive narration, one must also ask: What role does historical precedent play in Christian doctrine or the understanding of Christian experience? It should be noted that almost all biblically oriented Christians tend to treat precedents' normative authority to some degree or another, but it is seldom done with consistency. We tend to follow some narratives as establishing obligatory patterns, while neglecting others. For example, some churches have adopted three ordinances: Baptism, the Lord's Supper, and Foot Washing. Most churches follow the first two, but not the last. Those who do practice foot washing take the story in John 13 as normative for them to observe, following the example of Jesus and His disciples. Those who do not practice foot washing believe that Jesus told His disciples to follow His example of servanthood, but that this was not a command for believers to reproduce this particular act of servanthood. Although foot washing was a common and necessary custom of Jesus' day, it is not practiced in modern societies today. Nevertheless, the attitude of servanthood is still to be followed in the form appropriate to the situation.

Question #6: What are the limits of this text?

When interpreting a text, there is always a temptation to say more than is there. It is all right to acknowledge that there are limits to revelation and be content to admit ignorance of information that is beyond the text. If the Bible is silent on a subject, that is also for a reason. There are some things that God just did not tell us. Remember, the Bible was written to help us have a relationship to God. It was not intended to be a scientific book, a history of the world, or even a detailed explanation of why God does the things He does. It gives us all the information we need for our spiritual well-being and challenges us to put our faith in God. For those who have "inquiring minds," they will need to wait until God reveals all in eternity.

The Bible gives us all the information we need for our spiritual well-being and challenges us to put our faith in God.

The Second Coming of Christ is one topic people abuse by saying more than is given in the Bible. We are told that Christ is coming again (1 Thessalonians 4:13–18; Titus 2:12, 13), but not the exact time He is coming. Jesus commented on His return: "But of that day and hour no one knows, not even the angels in heaven, nor the Son, but only the Father" (Mark 13:32). Jesus admitted that He did not know the time of His return, yet people continually think they have found the answer to that question. Interestingly enough, the answer has been revised time and again, as predictions come and go without being fulfilled. Stay clear of saying more than the Bible tells us, and be content in the revelation we have been given.

9

∞

QUESTIONS FOR PERSONAL APPLICATION

"Therefore whoever hears these sayings of Mine, and does them, I will liken him to a wise man who built his house on the rock: and the rain descended, the floods came, and the winds blew and beat on that house; and it did not fall, for it was founded on the rock."

Matthew 7:24, 25

The most important step in Bible study is application. You cannot apply what you don't know, so study is important. But you can know the truth of God's Word and still choose not to obey it. We can do very thorough exegesis, analyzing the text with great accuracy. Yet life transformation comes when we respond to the God of the universe and apply the truth to our lives.

Question #1: What did God say to me today?

Take seriously what you have learned through your Bible study. When we say, "God spoke," we are not talking about an audible voice from the clouds or mysterious writing on the wall. We are talking about God communicating information to your life. We are all aware that humans communicate to each other in many different ways: the audible voice, the written word, sign language, touch, a look. It is amazing how a wife can simply look at her husband across a crowded room and he knows exactly what she is thinking: *I want to leave, I am not feeling well,* or most likely, *That is your third piece of cake!* The point is this, if we have many ways to communicate to one another, how many more ways can the God of the universe communicate to us? Yet the primary way in which He does is through the Bible. His Spirit will take the words and bring them to life, fill them full of meaning, impress them upon your heart, and make a direct application to your life.

If God chooses to impress upon you a significant truth, write it down and meditate on it. When you go to school or to a lecture, you take notes when the speaker says something significant. How much more ought we to write down what we learn from God? The first thing you must do is to capture that truth and process it. Take time and ask the Holy Spirit to help you understand what you have just learned. Remember, you are in the process of being shaped by God, and what you learn today will impact what happens tomorrow.

Consider the disciples in Mark 6. Jesus had just done a great miracle, feeding five thousand with five loaves of bread and two fish. Immediately after that miracle, Jesus sent them across the sea by themselves while He remained in prayer. A storm arose, the disciples began to fear, and Jesus came walking on the water. Now their fear turned to terror, supposing that Jesus was a ghost. Jesus, however, calmed the winds and eased their fear. Then there is an interesting statement: "They were greatly amazed in themselves beyond measure, and marveled. For they had not understood about the loaves, because their heart was hardened" (Mark 6:51, 52). In other words, they had not processed the last thing Jesus had done, and now they were disoriented to what He was currently doing in their midst. Every time God shows you something in His Word, take time to meditate on it. He is preparing you for what He is about to do.

> *Remember, you are in the process of being shaped by God, and what you learn today will impact what happens tomorrow.*

Question #2: What is the general principle for all believers?

You are not alone in your pursuit of God. He has given us all timeless truth that will benefit our life and our relationship to Him. Though we all have a personal relationship with God, our faith is also corporate. That is, there are general principles given to all who are in a covenant relationship with God. They show us how to live a good life in right standing with God and one another. When applied to our lives, we will experience life as God intended.

Jesus gave a powerful principle in Matthew 6:14, 15: "For if you forgive men their trespasses, your heavenly Father will also forgive you. But if you do not forgive men their trespasses, neither will your Father forgive your trespasses." The principle is clear: If we want God's forgiveness, we must also show forgiveness to others. Once we come to know God and experience His goodness in our lives, we must in return show that same goodness toward others. In other words, God will treat us in the same manner we treat others; the measure with which we treat others will be measured back to us. The application of this principle is that Christians should freely extend forgiveness to one another. As we forgive others of their sins toward us, God will forgive us of our sins toward Him.

The principle is clear, yet many don't understand it or even believe it. Although they ask God to forgive them of their sins, still they refuse to forgive others. The result: they become bitter, angry, and frustrated. They lose the joy of salvation, and their relationship with God seems distant. Why? When they asked God to forgive their sin, they assumed that He did. In reality, every time they asked forgiveness, He said "NO." They are living their lives under the false assumption that their relationship with God is in good standing, when, in fact, they still carry their sin and it has become a barrier between them and God. Whether we live by the principles in the Bible or not, rest assured, God does. We experience abundant life when we understand those principles and then apply them to our lives.

Question #3: What is the specific application to my life?

It is one thing to understand the general principles that God has given us; it is another thing to specifically apply them in real-life situations. God gives us more than general principles to follow; He shows us where and when to apply them. Once you learn the truth, ask the Holy Spirit to show you what to do about it. Ask Him to work it into your life and make it real.

Take, for example, the principle of forgiveness just mentioned above. The Holy Spirit will show you the truth about forgiveness, and then He will show you the person you need to forgive. Oftentimes, you have moved on in life, not knowing you needed to forgive. Other times, you know exactly who has hurt you and you refuse to show forgiveness to them. You justify, "they hurt me," "they don't deserve it," or "it's too late now." Then the Holy Spirit reminds you of God's grace in your own life. You hurt the Lord, you didn't deserve forgiveness, and God never gave up on you. He forgave you, and you need to forgive others, not because they deserve it, but because you didn't deserve it when God forgave you. Rest assured of this: the Holy Spirit will be very specific when applying biblical principles to your life.

There are four areas in which the Holy Spirit will apply a truth. Ask the Holy Spirit to show you how the truth impacts 1) your relationship to God, 2) your own personal life, 3) your relationship to other people, and 4) your involvement in the church. All four areas must be considered when applying the Bible to your life.

Question #4: Am I going to do it?

Up until now, everything has all been talk and good intentions. You need to *do* what God has said in His Word. This step is both the simplest and the hardest. You know what to do; you just need to do it. Many, however, have the same sentiment as did Mark Twain: what troubles us most is not that we don't understand what the Bible says, but that we do understand what it says. Obeying God and following His Word will inevitably mean humbling yourself, denying yourself, and making costly sacrifices.

This is the moment that reveals your relationship to Christ. Jesus said, "If you love Me, keep My commandments" (John 14:15). The Scripture also says, "This is the love of God, that we keep His commandments. And His commandments are not burdensome" (1 John 5:3). No matter what we say, our obedience reveals our love for God. When we respond to God out of a love relationship, His commands are no longer a burden.

> *When we respond to God out of a love relationship, His commands are no longer a burden.*

We mentioned in "Personal Preparation" (chapter 7) the importance of having a heart of ready obedience. Before you open God's Word and ask Him to guide your life, make the decision that you will obey Him before you ever hear Him speak. And when you have heard Him and clearly know what is required of your life, do it. Don't hesitate, but trust that God knows best and you can trust Him. As James 1:22 says, "Be doers of the word, and not hearers only, deceiving yourselves."

Question #5: Who will hold me accountable?

Once you know what God has said and you are committed to obey, you may need to share it with somebody else. Satan desires to weaken us through isolation; God desires to strengthen us through interdependence. Your walk with God is personal, but not private. God has no orphans; He intends that you live your life among the family of God. We need each other! We are challenged in Hebrews 10:24, 25, "Let us consider one another in order to stir up love and good works, not forsaking the assembling of ourselves together, as is the manner of some, but exhorting *one another*, and so much the more as you see the Day approaching."

When it comes to sharing with others what God has said in your time of Bible study, you need to pray and ask His guidance. There are times that God intends that you process a truth alone with Him—that you meditate quietly and seek Him in times of personal growth. He doesn't want you to seek advice from others prematurely, but to wait patiently before Him and process the truth. Then there are times when He wants you to share with other people who will both encourage and challenge you. He may bring along a mature believer who can help you understand and apply the truth to your life. You are connected to the body of Christ, and others are placed in your life for a reason. Allow others to be involved in your life; allow others to hold you accountable to what you know the Lord has said to you.

CHAPTER

10

⊗

ENCOUNTERING
TRUTH

Then Jesus said . . . , "If you abide in My word, you are
My disciples indeed. And you shall know the truth, and
the truth shall make you free."

John 8:31, 32

TRUTH IS PERSONAL

The world in which we live promotes a philosophy that cannot accept absolute truth; everything is relative. What is right
for you is not necessarily right for someone else. Of course,
that is the product of human reasoning, not biblical revelation. The Bible describes what is right to God and, therefore,
what is right for us. Truth, as described in the Bible, is not so

much a concept but a Person. Jesus said, "I am the way, the truth, and the life. No one comes to the Father except through Me" (John 14:6). Jesus is truth. When He speaks, you know the truth, and the truth will set you free.

When Jesus said, "truth shall make you free," He was not talking about knowledge or a concept. He was saying that freedom comes in a person's life as he or she walks in an intimate relationship with Him. *He* is truth, and His presence in your life will make all the difference. If you want to know the truth about any situation, you need to hear from Him. He is God and not only knows all things; He is in control of all things. Circumstances can often be confusing, but He brings an eternal perspective.

Take, for example, the story in Mark 4:35–41 of Jesus and His disciples crossing the Sea of Galilee. As they sailed across the water, Jesus decided to take a nap. On the journey, however, a storm began to brew; and the disciples became fearful. They awoke Jesus and cried, "Teacher, do You not care that we are perishing?"

If you were to ask them what the truth of that situation was, what would they say? They would see the waves getting higher, the wind getting stronger, the boat filling with water, and the situation quickly deteriorating. Their conclusion: "We perish!" Did they? No! This situation actually became the opportunity to know more about Jesus than they had ever known before. Truth was asleep in the back of the boat. Once Jesus stood up and spoke, then they knew the truth of the situation. When the created universe obeys His commands, it is obvious that no circumstance is beyond His control. So no matter what your circumstance in life might be, until you hear a word from Jesus, you don't know the truth. Never

determine truth without first consulting Him, for your circumstances do not control your life: He does. That is why a
consistent study of God's Word is so important in our lives: it
is through His Word that the Lord guides us.

TRUTH IS RELATIONAL

It is helpful to know that the Lord is more interested in your
relationship than your circumstances. In fact, He may alter
your circumstances in order to enhance your relationship.
Let's stay with our example of the disciples in the storm. They
were in their situation in the first place because they had
obeyed Jesus. He had told them to get in the boat and cross
over to the other side. You could say that *obedience to Jesus* put
them in harm's way. But how else would the disciples learn
about His power over the wind and the sea? In dramatic fashion, Jesus showed them truth; He is master over nature.

That truth, however, was discovered through relationship. If they had not been with Him, if they had not had a
relationship with Him, if they had not turned to Him for help
. . . they would have never known the truth. Those who don't
know Jesus cannot know absolute truth, because they are not
in a relationship to the One who reigns over all things and
can alter them according to His will. But those who are Christians can have access to heavenly wisdom through their relationship to Jesus Christ. He will often take you through chal-
lenging circumstances in order to show you truth about
Himself. That is what He wants you to know more than any
other thing.

When you open the Bible, consider your time with God from His perspective. Yes, you have things that you want to achieve and insights you want to gain. But if Bible study truly is an interaction between you and your Lord, there may be things He wants to initiate in your life. Always keep in mind that His greatest desire is that you know Him. He will lead you from that perspective, guiding you into a deeper relationship with Himself. It is in that relationship that you will know truth, and truth will set you free. Logic and understanding do not determine obedience; obedience comes from a relationship. So don't multitask with God. When you are spending time with Him, be all there; give Him your full attention.

> *[God's] greatest desire is that you know Him. He will lead you from that perspective, guiding you into a deeper relationship with Himself. It is in that relationship that you will know truth, and truth will set you free.*

TRUTH IS FREEDOM

As you are confronted with truth in the Bible, you are confronted with Christ's right to be Lord. He desires to set you free from sin and bring you into abundant life in Him (John 10:10). That freedom comes when you die to self and allow

Him to live in you. This discussion may seem out of place in a book on "studying the Bible," yet we must keep in mind the purpose of the Bible: it is a primary means for experiencing God in your life. Every time you confront God in the Bible, He will be moving you toward this end.

We have briefly looked at Jesus' statement to His disciples in John 8:32, "You shall know the truth, and the truth shall make you free." But let's consider the verses that follow. The disciples did not understand what Jesus was talking about. They saw themselves as proud descendants of Abraham, not as slaves in need of freedom. But Jesus said, "Most assuredly, I say to you, whoever commits sin is a slave of sin. And a slave does not abide in the house forever, *but* a son abides forever. Therefore if the Son makes you free, you shall be free indeed" (John 8:34–36). Jesus here clarifies His earlier statement. He makes a shift from "truth" setting a person free to the "Son" setting them free.

The apostle Paul recognized that "knowing Jesus" was the greatest pursuit of his life (Philippians 3:7–11). As a Pharisee, he had studied the Scriptures as a discipline—as a book to enhance his knowledge of God. But when he met Christ, everything changed. The more he knew Christ, the more he understood freedom. Christ set him free from the power of sin and death, so that he no longer feared either one. He declared, "For to me, to live *is* Christ, and to die *is* gain" (Philippians 1:21). That is freedom!

The great need of all people is freedom from sin and its deadening effect upon our spirit. Is there any greater need? Of all the interests that you might have, this is the Lord's great interest—setting people free. So as you study the Bible, keep this thought in the forefront. Truth sets you free; Jesus sets you free. Most of the time, we are like the Israelites who didn't think they needed freedom; most of the time we are wrong. Jesus wants to release us from that which will hold us back and rob us of abundant life in Him. Bible study, therefore, is a significant lifelong pursuit. It is a light to our path that brings us into a deeper relationship with God.

Can you see that the entire exercise of Bible study has a greater purpose than you first understood? The personal preparation, the interpretation of the text, the application, and the encounter with God—all of it is to set you free through a relationship to Jesus Christ. In that relationship, He will guide you through life and on into eternity with Him. Different parts of the Bible will give you different insights into that relationship. All of it was given for that purpose. So as you go through the next section on "Styles of Literature," prepare to encounter God differently as He is expressed through those various styles.

11

❦

STYLES OF LITERATURE

God, who at various times and in various ways spoke in time past to the fathers by the prophets, has in these last days spoken to us by His Son.

Hebrews 1:1, 2

IN VARIOUS WAYS

The Bible is a collection of written literature composed of prose and poetry. Under the inspiration of God, the writers utilized various styles of literature to convey truth to their audiences. Because each style of writing uniquely expresses truth, it is important to understand what type of literature you are reading for correct interpretation. Understanding the type of literature will open up new insights into the text and will inspire new appreciation of books of the Bible that may have seemed confusing or less interesting than other books. There is a saying that "all scripture is inspired by God, but some books are more inspired than others." We know that this is not true, but what is often meant by this expression is that some books are more enjoyable to read than others. Remember that God is the One who inspired the writers of Scripture. We can assume that He also is pleased with the style of literature in which the writers conveyed His message.

Think about your own experiences in life. There are times when you need to hear something plain and simple: "Just give me the facts!" Yet there are other times that you are touched deeply through a message given through music: O how the heart longs to sing, for music touches a place that words alone cannot find. Then there are the times when your creative imagination needs to be set free: you yearn for something beyond your day-to-day experiences— for a place where you can express yourself in a newly perceived reality. And who can go through life without ever sharing a heart-to-heart with a close friend through personal notes and letters? Consider, too, the time-honored tradition of storytelling. People just like a good story, as evidenced by the publishing and entertainment industries, which give us novels and movies as fast as they can be produced.

You will find in the Bible every form of literature that touches the hearts of men and women: plainly written history, music that stirs the soul, imaginative and fantastic imagery, letters to friends, and lots of great stories. The Bible communicates in a way that meets you where you are. In chapters 12—18, we will walk you through the literary styles you will study in the Bible. You will be given the tools to interpret the text, but also listen to your heart. God will communicate uniquely through the styles with which He has chosen to deliver His message.

Before we launch into the various styles, however, let's consider several characteristics of the text itself. First, the accuracy of the Bible is phenomenal when compared to most ancient texts. There are over 5,500 copies in existence that contain all or part of the New Testament. Most ancient documents were rarely, if ever, translated into other languages. Yet, at an early date, the New Testament was translated; over 18,000 other versions have been recovered. The early church fathers (before A.D. 325) quoted the Scriptures in their writings over 86,000 times. This may not impress you at first; but when compared to other ancient manuscripts, if a classical work has twenty copies, it is considered to be a great number. Of all the literature that comes from antiquity, the Bible stands alone in its faithful representation of the original documents.

A second feature of biblical literature that is found in every style is the realism of the text. Like it or not, the Bible shows the good, the bad, and the ugly; it is a very frank book. It does not cover up people's mistakes, but shows real people as they relate to God and to one another. Human weaknesses of biblical heroes are not covered up, but have been recorded for all to see. Prominent disciples argue, struggle with doubt, and even give up hope. The Bible deals with uncomfortable issues like sex, sin, and the facts of life. But it is for this very reason that this Book is considered inspired by God because any human writing a document for the purposes of gaining a following would not have included such flawed characters. This is not a man-made book, but an inspired Book about real people in relationship to their God.

So as you work through the text of the Bible, remember this important truth. The Bible deals with reality. The text you are studying was forged in real-life circumstances and was accurately preserved for our benefit.

The Bible deals with reality. The text you are studying was forged in real-life circumstances and was accurately preserved for our benefit.

Even though it was written many years ago in "ancient times," God will touch you today through the pen of our spiritual forefathers.

12

❧

OLD TESTAMENT POETIC LITERATURE

Bless the LORD, O my soul;
And all that is within me, bless His holy name!

Psalm 103:1

*P*oetic literature can be found in every book of the Bible. There are books that are typically designated as "poetic books" such as Psalms, Song of Solomon, and Lamentations; other books contain sections of poetry or use figurative language. It has been said that poetry speaks to the mind through the heart. Through vivid images and poetic devices, we encounter God in an emotional arena that is innate to our human nature. One must be careful, therefore, not to "overexegete" or to extract precise meaning out of every word and take its meaning beyond where the poet intended to go. He may have just painted a word picture to elicit an emotion, not to state a doctrinal position. Since poetry has its own unique set of rules, having some basic information on this type of literature will be very helpful as you encounter it in the Bible.

NOTABLE CHARACTERISTICS

Because poetry is used throughout the Bible, it is important to know how to recognize and interpret this type of literature. You may be wondering, *How do I do that?* Poetry is characterized by short, concise, and highly structured sentences. In comparison to a narrative passage, poetry tries to "tighten" the sentences and use fewer words. *Concise statements* are a characteristic to look for in poetry. For example, notice how the poet expresses his thoughts on personal sin, using only eleven words:

> If You, LORD, should mark iniquities,
> O Lord, who could stand? (Psalm 130:3)

His meaning is far reaching. He proclaims that every person is guilty of sin and is accountable to God. In addition, he points out that if God were to hold every sin against us and treat us according to what we deserve, no one would stand a chance.

Poets have often been compared to artists who draw a picture for their audience with words. *Word pictures* are a prominent tool of the poet. Rather than simply stating that a person who relies on the Lord will be strengthened, the poet exclaims, "They shall mount up with wings like eagles" (Isaiah 40:31). Instead of writing that nations of the earth can't compare to

God, the poet writes, "Behold, the nations *are* as a drop in a bucket, and are counted as the small dust on the scales" (Isaiah 40:15). Word pictures are given to express the truths of God. They draw out emotion from the audience and provide images that go beyond the words.

Parallelism is the most common characteristic of Hebrew poetry; it is its most notable structure. This is where a thought is expressed on one line, followed by a parallel thought on the next line. There are three basic types of parallelism used in Hebrew poetry. The first is called "synonymous parallelism" (similar thoughts), which is the repetition of the same idea in consecutive lines or verses. The poet says the same thing two different ways:

They will call on me, but I will not answer;

They will seek me diligently, but they will not find me. (Proverbs 1:28)

The heavens declare the glory of God;

And the firmament shows His handiwork. (Psalm 19:1)

The second type is called "synthetic parallelism" (additional thoughts) where the next line is used to develop, expand, or intensify a truth in a series of lines. The poet gives some additional information that both clarifies and enhances the first line:

Be master over your brethren,

And let your mother's sons bow down to you. (Genesis 27:29)

He has not dealt with us according to our sins,

Nor punished us according to our iniquities. (Psalm 103:10)

Parallelism, however, is not restricted to supporting or strengthening a thought. The third type is called "antithetic parallelism" (opposing thoughts), which is used to contrast two ideas:

Those who are of a perverse heart *are* an abomination to the LORD

But *the* blameless in their ways *are* His delight. (Proverbs 11:20)

A wise son makes a glad father,

But a foolish son *is* the grief of his mother. (Proverbs 10:1)

Within parallelism, the poet often uses words that are commonly associated together to express his message. For example, night / day, sickness / health, silver / gold, or wise / foolish can tie consecutive lines together and convey a simple message:

How often they provoked Him in the wilderness,

And grieved Him in the desert! (Psalm 78:40)

At times, the poet can use this structure to pose a question or leave the reader with a question concerning the first line. Notice how the following verse will provide an answer or reason for the declaration found in the first line:

"Sing to the LORD,

For He has triumphed gloriously!

The horse and its rider

He has thrown into the sea!" (Exodus 15:21)

OTHER POETIC DEVICES

Poetry uses figurative devices such as simile, metaphor, analogy, and personification to express ideas. Simile is a comparison of unlike things introduced by the word "like" or "as." Metaphor uses a word or phrase in the place of another to suggest a likeness. Analogy is a comparison based on likeness, and personification gives personal qualities especially to an abstraction or thing. These poetic devices serve to illustrate and express truths in a way that appeals to the reader's imagination. When approaching this type of literature, be careful to recognize when figurative speech is being used to make a point and do not interpret it literally. For example, Psalm 36:7 compares people trusting in God to a chick seeking protection under the wings of its mother: "Therefore the children of men put their trust under the shadow of Your wings." The passage simply, yet eloquently, describes the comfort and safety that is found under the protection of God. Consider the psalmist's words in Psalm 130:6:

My soul *waits* for the Lord

More than those who watch for the morning—

Yes, more than those who watch for the morning.

In this psalm, the poet describes how he cries out to God from *the depths*. The psalmist has been overwhelmed with the fact that his sin has separated him from God. He describes himself as waiting for God's forgiveness, knowing that this forgiveness will rescue him from *the depths*. His comparison is to a watchman who is guarding the walls during the night season. At night, the watchman has to strain his eyes to guard his post. The night provides a cover for the enemy that will disappear in the daylight. The reader can relate the anticipation the watchman has as he waits for the sunrise to the hope he feels in waiting for God's forgiveness.

The poets were able to create word pictures to make their points "stick" with their audience. Think about some of the common word pictures in the Scriptures. Isaiah 40:31 is a great example: "But those who wait on the LORD shall renew *their* strength; they shall mount up with wings like eagles." Psalm 1:3 describes the person who delights in the law of the Lord as being "like a tree planted by the rivers of water, that brings forth its fruit in its season, whose leaf also shall not wither." Both of these illustrations provide strong mental images that the reader can easily understand.

Oftentimes, we are familiar with the beautiful word pictures of God and memorize those that describe His help and provision. Poetry, however, is also used throughout the Bible to express God's hatred of sin and His wrath toward those who continue to ignore His warnings. At times, we can be overwhelmed with how poetry is used to express God's displeasure toward people. A poignant example is found in Isaiah 33:10–12

"Now I will rise," says the LORD;

"Now I will be exalted,

Now I will lift Myself up.

You shall conceive chaff,

You shall bring forth stubble;

Your breath, *as* fire, shall devour you.

And the people shall be *like* the burnings of lime;

Like thorns cut up they shall be burned in the fire."

GENERAL GUIDELINES

Always remember that a poem was meant to be read in its entirety, and strive to keep the total message of the poem in mind as you read. In addition, look for any use of parallelisms because the poet will use this structure to help support the main theme of the poetry. Finally, don't forget to locate and visualize figures of speech in the text and to recognize the emotion that is "stirred" from them.

Poetic language expresses ideas, feelings, and truths differently from prose. Don't assume that the literal meaning is the correct one. For example, when Isaiah addressed the people of Judah, he stated, "Hear the words of the LORD, you rulers of Sodom; give ear to the law of our God, you people of Gomorrah" (Isaiah 1:10). Sodom and Gomorrah were not in existence at this time. The prophet was comparing the wickedness of the people of Judah to the wickedness of these two cities that were notorious for their debauchery.

Remember that much of Hebrew poetry was written to music and performed (sung) rather than read. We do not have the music that accompanied the poetic literature, but we can still enjoy the beauty of this literature and let the words of the poets bring forth the images and emotions that were intended. This type of literature is a favorite for devotional reading, but don't use it merely as a way to start the day with a "good feeling." God is the One who is speaking; and anytime He speaks, you need to listen and take heed, considering where you should be applying His message to your daily life.

CHAPTER

13

❦

OLD TESTAMENT PROPHETIC LITERATURE

He has shown you, O man, what is good; and what does the LORD require of you but to do justly, to love mercy, and to walk humbly with your God?

Micah 6:8

A CLEAR MESSAGE FROM GOD

Throughout the history of Israel and Judah, God called individuals and set them apart as prophets. Their primary responsibility was to proclaim God's words to His people. Very simply, prophets were used to remind the people of their covenant responsibilities that had been given through Moses (Deuteronomy 4 and following). In addition, they were to proclaim God's words of repentance and forgiveness or judgment to the people of God. The prophets stood out more prominently as the champions of God's Word than any other group in Israel including the priests, kings, and wise men of their day. There were prophets throughout the entire history of Israel; however, it was only toward the later period (beginning in the eighth century B.C. and ending in the fifth century B.C.) that their messages and activities were recorded into prophetic books.

THE INTENSITY OF THE MESSAGE

The prophetic books are marked by strong language, colorful imagery, emotion-laden sentences, and enormous words of judgment and punishment.

At times, the continued words of judgment seem to "go on and on." It is important to remember that God called a prophet to proclaim His message as a last line of action before the judgment. God does not desire that anyone should perish, "'for I have no pleasure in the death of one who dies,' says the Lord GOD. 'Therefore turn and live!'" (Ezekiel 18:32). Hence, when you are reading the prophets, you are catching the last effort of God to bring His

When you are reading the prophets, you are catching the last effort of God to bring His people back to a relationship of love with Himself.

people back to a relationship of love with Himself. Another way to view this is that after repeated attempts to get the people to return to God, the "volume" is turned all the way up in order to get their attention.

The message of each prophet was essentially the same; it cycled throughout the history of God's people on a regular basis. Unfortunately, the people regularly neglected the covenant and needed a prophet to show them their sin and bring them back to the relationship. God had a purpose for His people. It was through them that He would redeem the entire world, yet they would fall into sin or adopt false gods and be of no use to Him whatsoever. Every time they would depart, the discipline of God would come upon the nation. As His discipline increased, the people would cry out to God for help. It was at this point that they had the chance to either repent or face judgment. This was the moment that the prophets delivered God's message. The message had the following elements: 1) Recognize your sin; 2) Repent of your sin and return to the covenant relationship with God; 3) If you refuse to repent, judgment is coming; and 4) There is a future hope of a Messiah who will restore the relationship with a new covenant.

THE SETTING FOR THE MESSAGE

One key to understanding a prophetic book is to determine the setting in which it was proclaimed. The prophetic literature provides hints to the time period and the location in which the prophet announced his message. Many of the prophets' ministries overlap and provide insight into the general social conditions of a particular time period. The fine details of the setting, however, may not be as readily available. Study Bibles often provide a brief introduction to each of the prophetic books, but the limited amount of space given to these introductions is not adequate for explaining the dynamics of the prophetic setting. A Bible atlas or brief history of Israel will help at this point. If you don't possess physical copies of these resources (in either print or electronic form), you may want to try gathering information on a book's setting from resources in your church library or through the Internet. This does not mean that you can't understand a prophetic book apart from an understanding of the surrounding history of Israel and Judah, but you may miss some of the details and connections within the book. For example, the books of Isaiah and Amos speak against the nations that surround Israel and Judah. It is not necessary to have a full understanding of each of these nations, but some knowledge of these kingdoms such as general locations, relationships to Israel and Judah, and current events surrounding the prophecy afford valuable insights into the text.

WORD PICTURES AND ACTIONS

The prophets drew upon vivid word pictures and analogies to convey God's message to the people. When God called Jeremiah to deliver the message to "root out and to pull down, to destroy and to throw down, to build and to plant" (Jeremiah 1:10), the Lord told the young prophet not to be dismayed for

He had made him "a fortified city and an iron pillar, and bronze walls against the whole land" (Jeremiah 1:18). Speaking through the prophet Amos, God announced that He is "setting a plumb line in the midst of My people Israel" (Amos 7:8) for the purpose of holding them accountable. The use of these analogies added force and made the images stay with its listeners. Be careful to spend time picturing the images and analogies used in the prophetic material to bring insight into the messages presented.

Be careful to spend time picturing the images and analogies used in the prophetic material to bring insight into the messages presented.

At times, God called the prophets to physically act out His message to the people—a unique method of delivery you may find radical. For example, when you come across God's instructions for Ezekiel to perform the siege of Jerusalem (Ezekiel 4) or the sword coming against the city (Ezekiel 5), recognize this radical effort was often the last warning extended to the people before final judgment. While many of the actions seem odd, they served to present a physical example of coming judgment. Remember, their purpose was to awaken the people and cause them to repent.

If you find yourself becoming overwhelmed with the word pictures, symbolism, and actions of the prophets, simply take a step back and let the Holy Spirit apply the broader principles of the text to your life. Make sure you apply the questions for textual interpretation and allow the Bible to be its own commentary. If you still are left confused, don't force a meaning into the text; be patient for the Holy Spirit to guide you. You can trust that if you spend time reading through and studying the prophetic literature, the Spirit will be faithful to open your understanding and apply truth to your life.

SMALL BITES AT A TIME

The larger prophetic books are collections of prophecies given over many years of ministry and can be difficult to understand as a whole. These books were not spoken in a single setting, nor were they intended to be understood as a whole in the way that a letter from the apostle Paul to a New Testament church would have been read. Read these books in small sections (such as a section of verses, a chapter, or a grouping of chapters). As you read, look for the major truths in the smaller sections and link them to the overall theme of the book.

ILLUSTRATION

Let's take a look at one of the great passages from the eighth-century prophets in **Micah 6:6–8.**

Background

Because the messages of the prophets are so closely tied to the specific events of the day in which they spoke, it is helpful to have access to a Bible atlas that includes a brief history of

Israel and Judah. Micah 1:10–16 most likely described the military campaign of the Assyrian king Sennacherib from Lachish to Jerusalem in 701 B.C., thus providing the setting for the prophecy. The cultural setting is provided throughout the book where Micah speaks against the sins of the listeners. The sins of the people relate to two areas: 1) the perversion of their worship practices (1:7; 3:5–7; 5:11–14); and 2) injustice toward other people (2:1, 2, 8, 9; 3:2, 3, 9–11; 7:2–6).

A Lawsuit from God

Old Testament prophecy uses a variety of techniques to make its point to the audience. Micah 6:1–8 uses the image of a court of law. The lawsuit is presented by God, followed by a time of questioning. In 6:1–5, God makes known His grievance against His people, for they have broken the covenant that He established with them. With a brilliant use of language, God calls upon the created universe to witness the atrocity. The mountains and hills form the jury and hear God's case against Israel. Like a seasoned trial lawyer, God asks the question, "What fault has Israel found in God?" He then recounts His loving relationship to a people who have turned away. In comparison to His faithfulness to them, the sins of the nation appear as an abomination.

Transitions

Among the difficulties with understanding prophecy are the quick transitions from God speaking to the prophet speaking to the people responding. A passage can become very confusing if you do not look carefully for the transitions. Micah 6:6 is a transition from God's suit to the response of the people of Israel. Israel had displeased God, but she claimed ignorance and asked what she must do to be acceptable. Micah 6:6, 7 reveal that Israel continued to miss the mark with God. The people only looked to offer sacrifices, possessions, and good works. They gave lavish gifts to God without addressing the issues of corruption and injustice. Sacrifices were required according to Mosaic Law (Leviticus 1—6), but they were meaningless apart from a clean heart. Religious sacrifice was useless without a proper relationship to God and right living with one's neighbor.

Another transition occurs in Micah 6:8, where the prophet declared what God requires of the people—what it takes to be acceptable before Him. God desires worshipers who love God, serve God, and practice justice with other people. This is a message that is common throughout the prophets of the Old Testament. It is also spoken through Isaiah (Isaiah 1:1–17) and Amos (Amos 5:21–24).

Do the Prophets Have a Word for Us?

The message of the prophets is powerful, presented uniquely with stark contrasts and vivid pictures. Unlike some forms of biblical literature, the truths are presented in strong and emotional language. For the original audience the message was clear; the way they were living was a violation of the covenant relationship with God. He had held up His side of the covenant, but they had not lived up to the standard He had set for them. The prophet's words were a call to repent and live as the covenant people of God.

The prophetic theme, "to do justly, to love mercy, and to walk humbly with your God," echoes throughout the entire Bible, Old and New Testament alike. A passage spoken to people facing the threat of an Assyrian army during the eighth century B.C. also rings true in our day. He is justified in calling the earth as a witness against our lives, saying, "What fault have you found in God that you live the way you do?" Indeed, God has done immeasurably more than you could ask or think. The settings are different, but the vivid pictures of how God deals with His people quickly become personal under the guidance of the Holy Spirit.

14

☙

OLD TESTAMENT NARRATIVE LITERATURE

Now Naaman, commander of the army of the king of Syria, was a great and honorable man in the eyes of his master, because by him the LORD had given victory to Syria. He was also a mighty man of valor, but a leper.

2 Kings 5:1

THE STORY GOES LIKE THIS

About 40 percent of the Old Testament is narrative literature. Narrative is different from pure history in that the writer is not simply recounting information (names, dates, events), but rather is telling a story in order to convey specific truths to later generations. The writer is not trying to give a comprehensive account of an event, but to provide enough information to relate a reality of God to the reader. As with any good story, the writer makes use of description, plot, characterization, dialogue, wordplay, and other literary devices to engage the reader to listen and to learn the truths of God.

Do not become overwhelmed with the technical side of reading a narrative passage in the Bible. Not only is this style enjoyable to read, but the Holy Spirit will also use it to impress upon you significant insights into the nature of God. We will identify some of the literary features of narrative literature that will help you know what to look for when reading the Bible. We will then apply these basic tools to a passage of Scripture.

THINGS TO LOOK FOR

For the most part, what you are looking for in a narrative passage from the Bible is the same as what you look for in any good book or story: the story line/plot and the characters involved. In some cases, the plot and the main characters are very obvious and interesting (Exodus 2; 1 Samuel 15). Some narrative passages, however, tell of common events like a construction project (1 Kings 7:2–8) and do not capture our interest as readily nor do they contain much interaction between the characters of the story. So, depending on the story, the significance of its details may or may not be readily apparent.

Begin your study of a narrative book by looking for its *plot* or overall theme. The Bible is God-centered, and the narrative passages will in some way reveal the nature or ways in which God interacts with humankind. The main story line will unify the characters and events of the story around a central truth.

Narrative passages will in some way reveal the nature or ways in which God interacts with humankind.

Next, look at the *characters* who are involved in the story. A narrative does not attempt to give a comprehensive history of an event, but uses specific characters to make its point. Therefore, the characters involved and the interaction between them have been specially chosen to support the plot. Often, the people and their interaction provide numerous subplots within the narrative.

You must also take note of the *setting* of the narrative (time, place, current events). This will provide valuable insights into the life and actions of the people involved. For example, the setting for the prophet Elijah tells you that he was responding to the condition of Israel under the rule of King Ahab and the evil Phoenician queen Jezebel.

You will notice that the writers may even use a literary device called narrative *pacing*. We may better understand this term by watching a movie that starts off slowly, but that builds in suspense as the story line heads to the conclusion or final scene. Narrative often "builds suspense" to emphasize the main point or truth at the conclusion of the story. This can be done with descriptive wording, character interaction, or escalating conflict.

THE BIG PICTURE

Narrative passages are often part of a larger story or series of stories linked to themes found throughout an entire book. If you are reading a passage that focuses on a particular person such as Abraham, Moses, or Elijah, be careful to relate the passage to the overall account of this person's life. Take the truths that are presented in the passage and link them to the manner in which God walked with and used this individual for His purposes. The Bible must be considered in its entirety, and each story therefore gives input into the larger story line of God.

ILLUSTRATION

Now, let's look at a narrative passage from **2 Kings 5:1–27.**

Larger Context

The story takes place in the beginning chapters of 2 Kings where the material presents the ministry of Elisha the prophet. Elisha was used in Israel and in the surrounding countries as a champion of God. It is significant to note that the scriptures surrounding chapter 5 indicate that Israel and Syria were not on good terms and had a history of conflict. In fact, the beginning of the story recalls a recent Syrian raid on Israel that had involved the taking of at least one Israelite captive.

Plot

The central plot of the story is God bringing healing to Namaan. Looking more closely at the story, however, there are several theological subplots on the themes of conversion, monotheism (the understanding that there is only one God), the power of God's word, and the danger of coveting.

Following the main story, the reader encounters several significant developments in the plot: the role of a servant girl and her compassion for Naaman's condition; the king of Syria's letter and riches that were sent to obtain help; the troubled response of the king of Israel; Elisha's offer to help; the pride of Naaman at the requirements for healing; the servant's plea to Naaman; Naaman's healing and offer of payment to the prophet; and Gehazi's greed and subsequent punishment. All of these points can teach us a valuable lesson and are worthy of further examination.

Characters Involved

Naaman
- Leader of the Syrian army
- Held in high regard by the king of Syria
- A leper
- All of his power and wealth could not cure him; Naaman needed help from God

Servant Girl
- Her name is not given
- Noted as young, probably no more than a child

- Of low status (waited on Naaman's wife)

- Taken captive and away from her home and family but did not lose her trust in God, nor the courage to state the truth of her God

- Insignificant in people's eyes, but used by God to impact Naaman's life

The Kings

- Both characters acted like kings (if there is a problem, they bought or demanded a solution)

- They spoke to the earthly authorities and missed the truth that God is the One in control

Elisha

- Saw an opportunity to help Naaman so that he might come to know the true God

- Did not treat Naaman any differently based on his status

- Did not draw attention to himself and took no money for the miracle

Gehazi

- Filled with greed

- Disregarded the example and teachings of Elisha

Some General Observations

Now that we have discovered some of the general characteristics of the passage, it is time to look at what the writer was trying to teach through this narrative. It is always important to begin with the original audience that the writer was addressing before moving to any personal application for our day. The story of Naaman, like those of Ruth and Jonah, taught that God desired that all nations know Him. Jesus would later use this story as an example of God revealing Himself to those outside of Israel (Luke 4:27). The story also taught the importance of obedience to the prophetic word. Naaman was not healed when he washed in the Jordan because its waters were purer than the waters of Syria's rivers, but because of his obedience to God's words through the prophet. Gehazi, conversely, was punished for his disobedient move to cancel Elisha's oath. The story reveals that it was God and not the prophet who brought the healing, for the prophet did not even come into contact with Naaman until after the miracle was completed.

Applying the Story

You are not only attempting to gain understanding of the biblical times, but seeking the guidance of the Holy Spirit to apply the Word of God to your life. A thorough understanding of the passage simply provides the opportunity for the Spirit to "wield the Word of God" into your life. Some of the important themes found in this narrative include the following: 1) God pursues and orchestrates events to bring people to faith in Him; 2) obedience to the commands of God will bring healing and life; and 3) there are consequences to dishonest and greedy behavior.

We can look at overall themes, but a narrative also provides wonderful teachings through the use of its characters.

For example, *Naaman* almost missed God's healing because of his pride. He was expecting the kind of great healing that is "fitting" for a man of his stature (verses 11, 12). He wanted God's help, but wanted this help on his terms rather than on God's terms. Instead of being grateful for the chance of healing, he became angry at the prophet for not meeting with him personally. The example of Naaman's pride finds many connections to New Testament teachings on humbling oneself before the Lord.

The *Servant Girl* was taken captive from her native land and made a slave. She, however, neither lost her faith in Yawheh nor did she become bitter. In fact, when her captor became sick, she confidently informed Naaman that he could find healing from her homeland. She maintained a trust in God and continued to declare the might of her God. The example of this girl serves as a powerful testimony for any generation.

The *Prophet Elisha* did not touch the glory of the miracle God performed. He recognized that Naaman's healing was a free gift from God and refused to accept any payment. What is even more fascinating is that Naaman was a military leader from a country that was continually at war with Israel. Yet there was no hint of prejudice from the prophet. Rather, he demonstrated simple obedience to the work of the Lord.

YESTERDAY AND TODAY

Narrative literature provides valuable teaching about the nature of God and truths for all Christians to incorporate into their lives. It may take some energy to understand a narrative passage as you work through the plot and seek to understand the interplay between the characters and how they relate to God's plan. You will find, however, that it is well worth the effort. You may be thinking of some other stories in the Bible that, in the past, you have simply read as historical accounts of names, dates, and events. Return to these scriptures and let the Holy Spirit unfold the stories in a fresh and life-changing way. The stories of yesterday are very relevant to your life today.

CHAPTER

15

❧

NEW TESTAMENT
GOSPELS

*"It seemed good to me also, having had perfect under-
standing of all things from the very first, to write to you
an orderly account, most excellent Theophilus, that you
may know the certainty of those things in which you
were instructed."*

Luke 1:3, 4

Many people would describe the Gospels as their favorite part of the Bible. The life and ministry of Jesus is portrayed vividly through Matthew, Mark, Luke, and John. Here we read about miracles, radical healing experiences, and unprecedented teaching from the Lord. The Gospels are the first four books of the New Testament and can be divided into two groups. *The synoptic Gospels* (Matthew, Mark, and Luke) are one grouping, while the Gospel of John is viewed by itself. The word "synoptic" originates from a Greek word meaning "seeing together."

A quick read through Matthew, Mark, and Luke reveals numerous similarities. These books record many of the same events and teachings, use similar language or wording, and arrange events in the life of Jesus in a relatively corresponding order. Because of these common features, the books can be compared to each other to gain a more complete picture of events from the life of Jesus. For example, the beginning verses of Luke 5 record how Jesus called Peter and his fishing partners James and John into ministry with Him. In reading Matthew's account of this event, we become aware that Peter's brother Andrew was also called into ministry on this same occasion (Matthew 4:18–20).

While the Holy Spirit inspired Matthew, Mark, and Luke as they wrote their accounts, we must recognize that they describe the life and ministry of Jesus from different perspectives. In one sense, we can compare this to interviewing witnesses of a car crash. One witness may describe the direction of the oncoming car, but not include the type and color of the car. Another witness may not describe the cars or direction, but the condition of the occupants of the cars following the crash. A third witness may repeat much of the same information, but include the weather conditions that affected the crash. Each witness provides the information that he or she deems pertinent, and together they provide a full picture of the crash. Likewise, the synoptic Gospels provide a full picture of the ministry of Jesus Christ.

John's Gospel, however, is unique in comparison to the synoptic Gospels. Only about 10 percent of its content is "in common" with the other Gospels. For instance, the cleansing of the temple and the feeding of the 5,000 are included in all four Gospels, but events such as the Last Supper and the Transfiguration are not included in the Gospel of John. The Gospel of John does not include the Lord's teaching through parables or His use of short, poignant sayings. Instead, John makes use of longer sections of material such as the dialogue with Nicodemus (John 3), or the Upper Room Discourse (John 13—16) to present the Lord's teachings.

The synoptic Gospels stand apart from John in that they present the ministry of Jesus according to geographic region. They begin with His ministry in Galilee, Judea, and Perea, and conclude with His ministry in Jerusalem. John's Gospel does not report Jesus' ministry by region, but rather places heavy emphasis on the events that took place in Jerusalem.

GOSPELS AS LITERATURE

The word "gospel" means "good news" and was used in the early church to refer to the good news of the message of Jesus Christ. Once Matthew, Mark, Luke, and John had recorded their accounts of the ministry of the Lord, the early church began to refer to these accounts as the good news, or more specifically, as the gospel according to Matthew, Mark, Luke, and John. The Gospels do not "fit" neatly into any one category of literature. In part, they can be considered biographies of Jesus as they record His life and teachings. The comparison to a biography, however, must be very loose as Mark and John make no mention of Jesus' birth, childhood, or early adulthood. In fact, Luke and Matthew only make brief mention of events prior to His public ministry. The Gospels give the greatest attention to the last weeks and days of Jesus' life and do not attempt to provide an overview of His life as we would expect in a traditional biography. Perhaps the best way to describe the Gospels is as *theological biographies*.

The Gospels are unique. They include biographical material, but they serve to express the truth that God the Father was "in Christ" accomplishing His purposes to redeem humankind. The teachings of Christ are not simply to be read for information, but are to be studied with the expectation that the same Lord who taught these truths in Palestine is present today through the Holy Spirit. Most notably, the Gospels present theology and its practical application for followers of Christ.

Perhaps the best way to describe the Gospels is as theological biographies.

ONE AT A TIME

Each Gospel was written as an individual book. Each was written with a specific purpose and to a particular audience. The writers had individual rationales for the material they chose to include and for the specific themes they wanted to draw out in their material. Therefore, when you read a Gospel, be careful to look at a passage in light of the entire book before making comparisons to another Gospel. Look to see the major themes that are present in the individual

Gospels such as Matthew's continued emphasis on the transfer of the kingdom of Israel to the church or Luke's desire to show Jesus as a friend of those who were the marginalized in Jewish society (Samaritans, tax collectors, the poor, women, and Gentiles).

LITERARY FORMS TO LOOK FOR

Parables: Parables are stories that relate to common experiences of life. Their purpose is to catch the listener's attention and teach an underlying truth through the story. The effectiveness of these stories is evident as they are the most easily recognizable style of teaching in the Gospels. You may not be able to outline all of the various styles of teaching in the Gospels, but most likely you could name many parables such as "The Sower" (Matthew 13), "The Lost (or Prodigal) Son" (Luke 15), "The Lost Sheep" (Luke 15), "The Good Samaritan" (Luke 10), and "The Mustard Seed" (Matthew 13). As readers recall these stories, they will also remember their spiritual application and truths.

Parables are stories that catch the listener's attention and teach an underlying truth through the story.

Parables are used in the Gospels to reveal spiritual truth and their application to the Christian life. As with any good story, it is important to be mindful of the plot, characters, and contrast between the people or objects utilized. Each parable will have a main theme or truth that it is designed to teach. In some cases, there can be several important truths presented throughout the story. Discovering the main truth or truths in a parable is less difficult in the shorter parables such as "The Mustard Seed" or "The Leaven" (Luke 13:18–21). In longer parables, such as "The Lost Son" (Luke 15), there are several key truths related to repentance and forgiveness that can be quickly recognized. In addition to the main theme, the parable provides many insights into the Christian life. Remember that the parables were designed to relate to common issues of life. For example, most readers have found themselves connecting their life experiences to those of the characters found in the parable of the lost son. Many can relate to the wayward son, the angered brother, or the forgiving father. The description of the loving father also provides a picture of God the Father. The love that he has for his wayward son, the forgiveness he shows, and the lavish reception he provides upon this son's return, present a picture of God in relation to His people.

When you read a parable, be careful to look for the main theme or purpose of the story. In some cases, there may be more than one key truth. This truth is often presented through the contrast of two characters such as "The Pharisee and the Tax Collector" (Luke 18:9–14) or two groups of people such as "The Wise and Foolish Virgins" (Matthew 25:1–13). Also, look to see if the parable has been grouped together with other parables to enforce a common theme. For example, Matthew 24 begins with Jesus teaching on the end of the age and the return of the Son of Man. Following this teaching are the parables of "The Fig Tree," "The Faithful and the Evil Servants," "The Wise and Foolish Virgins," and "The Talents." These parables are grouped together with a common theme of being prepared for the return of the Lord.

Once you have determined the main point of the parable, remember that there are often secondary truths and applications that will give wonderful insight into your life and walk with God. You will find yourself identifying with characters in the parables and discovering fresh understandings of the nature and character of God and His kingdom.

Hyperbole: If you have children, you are probably familiar with the practice of using hyperbole to make your point. Have you ever found yourself saying, "I have told you a thousand times to clean your room"? You were not actually counting the number of times you talked to your kids about cleaning their rooms, but you wanted them to know that you were tired of asking them to do it. Or you may have used the expression "I almost died laughing" when, in fact, you were not even close to dying. You were simply trying to say that you thought something was very funny. A statement that is not literally true but that is exaggerated to make a point is called a hyperbole. The Gospels make use of hyperbole to drive a point home with the reader. This does not mean that there is any intentional misleading of the reader. The use of hyperbole was common in Jesus' day, and it continues to be used effectively today. It is important to recognize the use of hyperbole, though, and in turn to understand that hyperbolic statements should not be taken literally.

For example, in Matthew 5:27–30, Jesus addressed the sin of adultery in the heart (lust). Jesus spoke of the sin of looking at a woman with lust and made the statement in verse 29: "If your right eye causes you to sin, pluck it out and cast *it* from you; for it is more profitable for you that one of your members perish, than for your whole body to be cast into hell." Jesus was not saying that a person needs to literally cut his eye out to stop himself from lusting after a woman. A few verses before He had been teaching that sin is a matter of the heart. We can recognize that the act of plucking out the eye would not change the condition of one's heart. In addition, a person *lusting* would most likely not discriminate between which eye had looked at the person. We can assume that the person looked with both eyes (not simply with the right one); but in Jesus' day, the "right eye" was viewed as more valuable, and so His point was made even stronger.

Jesus employed hyperbole to give a strong warning about the danger of lust and the ruin it can bring to a person's life. Adultery is rarely a random act; it is preceded by first looking at someone, then having lustful thoughts, and finally acting on those lustful thoughts. Jesus commanded His hearers to take drastic measures to avoid temptations to sexual sins. In stressing His point, He said that anything that could cause one to sin should be completely removed.

Jesus often used hyperbole to stress the dangers of sin and its consequences.

Jesus often used hyperbole to stress the dangers of sin and its consequences. For example, the parable "The Faithful and the Evil Servants" makes use of this literary form to stress the seriousness of disobeying God: "The master of that servant will come on a day when he is not looking for *him* and at an hour that he is not aware of, and will cut him in two and appoint *him* his portion with the hypocrites" (Matthew 24:50, 51). Cutting the servant in two pieces should not be taken literally as the remainder of the verse indicates that the servant will be allotted his portion. The use of hyperbole in this instance served as a vivid warning of the way in which God views disobedience by His servants.

Miracles/Signs: The Gospels record Jesus performing many miracles throughout His ministry. Nowadays, when we come across a miracle in one of the Gospels, we might marvel at the power of God and then simply continue reading. Anytime you notice a miracle, recognize that the miracles were not an end in themselves, but always pointed to the identity of Jesus as the Christ. As you read the Gospels, be careful to understand why a Gospel has recorded a specific miracle and placed it in the text at that particular point. Ask yourself, "How does the miracle relate to the surrounding scriptures?" In addition, recognize that each of the Gospel writers utilized and recorded Jesus' miracles to emphasize different things.

For example, in Matthew's Gospel, many of the miracles were presented as the fulfillment of scriptures (1:21–23; 8:16, 17; 12:15–21). Matthew continually used the miracles to teach the people that the words of the prophets had been fulfilled in and through the life of Jesus.

Miracles also played a very important role in the Gospel of Mark. Here, they served to demonstrate the power of God working through Jesus as He announced the coming of the kingdom of God (1:29–34; 2:1–12; 3:1–6; 5:21–43; 6:30–52; 7:31–36; 8:22–26).

Luke's Gospel closely linked Jesus' teaching with His healing ministry. He recorded the miracles together with Jesus' teachings and used them to spread the Gospel message (4:18; 5:15; 6:17; 9:11).

John, on the other hand, referred to miracles as "signs" that point to the deity of Christ. John recorded only seven miracles (2:1–11; 4:46–51; 5:1–9; 6:16–21; 9:1–7; 11:1–44). It is important to note that each of these miracles is placed at the beginning of a long discourse emphasizing the identity of Christ and the importance of His message.

The miracles were used in all of the Gospels to announce the identity of the Lord, to emphasize that the power of God was upon Him and that the kingdom of heaven was at hand.

The miracles were used in all of the Gospels to announce the identity of the Lord, to emphasize that the power of God was upon Him and that the kingdom of heaven was at hand. When you come across a miracle in the Gospels, always recognize that each writer placed that miracle at that point for a very specific purpose. Always look at the miracles in light of the scriptures that are just before and after the miracle. Approaching miracles this way will give you a full picture of the writer's intent. After considering these things, look at the other Gospels where the miracle is recorded to gain the other writers' viewpoints. (A "Harmony of the Gospels" feature or cross-reference system will help you find the places in the Bible where these miracles are found.) Miracles are a vital part of each Gospel and should be approached, studied, and applied to the Christian's life.

> and that the
> kingdom of heaven
> was at hand.

16

THE BOOK OF ACTS: A THEOLOGICAL HISTORY

And the Lord added to the church daily those who were being saved.

Acts 2:47

$\mathcal{T}$he Book of Acts is unique among the literature of the New Testament because it provides a historical account of the first thirty years of the early church. Further, it is the only biblical source that outlines the establishment and growth of early Christianity. The book is divided into two sections with the first twelve chapters detailing the mission of the Jerusalem church and the remainder of the book describing the missionary work of the apostle Paul.

Acts was written as the second volume of a two-volume work alongside of the Gospel of Luke. They should be viewed as a two-volume set even though in our modern arrangement of the New Testament, they are separated by the Gospel of John. The first volume (the Gospel of Luke) is a theological biography of Jesus; the second volume (the Book of Acts) is a theological history of the early church. Although the book was probably untitled when it was written, it has been given the name "Acts" or "Acts of the Apostles." This name can be a little misleading, because the book does not provide information about all of the apostles of the early church. Acts does not offer detailed accounts of any of the disciples except Peter and Paul. John is only mentioned in a secondary role on three occasions while more consideration is given to Stephen and to Philip than to the rest of the apostles.

LUKE'S HISTORY

In order to understand the Book of Acts, it is important to realize Luke's rationale for writing this account. According to Luke 1:1–4, Luke created an orderly reckoning of the events surrounding Jesus and the early church so that the reader could know for certain that the events (many of which Luke actually witnessed) were true. What we find in the Book of Acts is an orderly history of the events of early Christianity. Luke takes greater effort than any other New Testament writer to connect the history of the expansion of the church to the larger context of world history. He mentioned the emperor Claudius; the Roman procurators and governors Gallio, Felix, and Festus; and the Jewish kings Herod Agrippa I and Herod Agrippa II. Luke was not, however, writing a history like those to which we are accustomed. He did not include information such as how the gospel came to Rome or Paul's establishment of the church at Colosse. He was very discriminating in what he included and was determined to give *selective glances* of the early church. Luke wanted to provide an edifying record of how Christianity moved from a small group of Jewish followers to the Gentile capital of Rome. The selective glances at these events are designed to encourage and instruct the reader to embrace this same missionary calling under the guidance of the Holy Spirit.

> *Luke wanted to provide an edifying record of how Christianity moved from a small group of Jewish followers to the Gentile capital of Rome.*

THE COMING OF THE HOLY SPIRIT

The Book of Acts records a turning point for Christianity. Chapter 1 announces Jesus' promise that the disciples would receive power from the Holy Spirit. This power would enable them to "be witnesses to Me in Jerusalem, and in all Judea and Samaria, and to the end of the earth" (Acts 1:8). Chapter 2 records the coming of the Holy Spirit at Pentecost, followed by a description of the demonstration of the power of the Spirit. Acts must be read with the understanding that at Pentecost the church was empowered by the Spirit to fulfill the command of God to spread the gospel. The Holy Spirit is mentioned more than fifty times throughout the Book of Acts. We will not provide every reference to the Spirit; but to give a brief picture, there is reference to the promise of the Spirit (2:33; 5:32), to baptism in the Spirit (1:5; 11:16), to the fullness of the Spirit (4:8; 6:3), to receiving the Spirit (8:15), to speaking by the Spirit (4:25; 21:4), and to the comfort of the Spirit (9:31). In reading the Book of Acts, always keep in mind that it was the empowerment of the Spirit that enabled the early church to maintain their unity, speak boldly, perform miracles, find strength and comfort, and join with God in His mission to spread the gospel.

LOOK FOR THE EPISODES

Remember that Luke was not presenting a complete history, but rather was presenting his material through select episodes of the Christian expansion. Therefore, once you have gained an overall picture of the book, go back and try to understand Acts by looking at each of the specific periods. The book can be divided into two main parts. The first twelve chapters address the Christian ministry to the Jews beginning in Jerusalem and moving out to Palestine and Syria. The second division describes the Christian ministry to the Gentiles; it encompasses Paul's missionary journeys, his trip to Jerusalem, and finally his time in Rome. Both of these main sections can be further divided into individual episodes.

Under the direction of the Holy Spirit, think through the importance of each section to understand its significance to the expansion of the church. Ask yourself, "What does an individual section reveal about the ways of God?" For example, Acts 6:1—9:31 provides the details of Stephen's martyrdom, Philip's missionary work, and Paul's conversion. This section provides an overall picture that shows how even under persecution, the early church expanded.

SPEECHES IN ACTS

The numerous speeches included in the text comprise one of the prominent characteristics of the Book of Acts. The speeches make up about 30 percent of the content of Acts. The longest speech is Stephen's address before his death (7:2–53). Three speeches by Peter are included (2:14–40; 3:12–26; 10:34–43). Luke also recorded missionary speeches from Paul (13:16–41; 17:22–31; 20:18–35) and speeches made for Paul's defense (22:1–21; 24:10–21; 26:1–29). Luke used the speeches to underscore the significance of the events and circumstances surrounding the lives of the church. In addition, the speeches provide much of the theological teaching in the book.

APPLYING ACTS

Remember, Acts presents a history of the how the early church advanced the gospel under the empowerment of the Holy Spirit. The teaching and spiritual application in Acts are less direct than in other books of the New Testament. Therefore, in reading the Book of Acts, it may seem that the truths of God that can specifically apply to your daily life may not "jump off the page" as they do when you read a book like Romans or Philippians. Acts does not contain sections of teaching or *commandments* that personally apply similar to those found in the Gospel of Matthew's "Sermon on the Mount." So look to see if there are specific themes that are carried throughout the book such as *being a faithful witness of Christ*. Acts binds together the understanding of true discipleship with that of being a faithful witness; Acts helps us understand a Christian's relationship to the world. We may not deal with the exact situations experienced by the early church, but we can draw from their testimony as we function within our own governmental systems. Themes such as the providence of God, the power of the Spirit, the impact of the gospel message, and the inclusiveness of salvation pro-

> *Acts is an encouragement to every Christian who has a heart to share the good news of Christ. . . . Any group of Christians empowered by the Spirit can and will transform their world.*

vide rich truths and application to every reader. Acts also gives the context for reading the epistles of the New Testament and offers additional insights into the lives of the Christians discussed in other New Testament books.

The closing words of the Book of Acts sum up the heart of the book: "Preaching the kingdom of God and teaching the things which concern the Lord Jesus Christ with all confidence, no one forbidding him" (Acts 28:31). Acts is an encouragement to every Christian who has a heart to share the good news of Christ. It depicts the gospel as triumphant in the face of enormous obstacles from within and without the church. The heart and courage of the early church continues to show churches today that any group of Christians empowered by the Spirit can and will transform their world.

17

☙

NEW TESTAMENT
EPISTLES

*Paul, an apostle of Jesus Christ by the will of God, and
Timothy our brother, to the saints and faithful brethren
in Christ who are in Colosse: Grace to you and peace
from God our Father and the Lord Jesus Christ.*

Colossians 1:1, 2

*E*pistles make up a majority of the New Testament
Scriptures. They are actually letters that were written
by the apostles and early church leaders to various
churches or individuals within the Christian community.
They are fascinating books that give us great insight into the
development of the early church. Through them, we get a
unique peek into the lives of the early Christians, viewing
both their struggles and their triumphs. We also watch how
the apostles processed the implications of the gospel story
and clarified theological truths.

There were two types of letters that were common during the New Testament period. The first was formal and artistic; the second was informal and personal. The New Testament epistles are distinct from these types of letters, as they tend to be less structured and less artistic than a formal letter, but longer and more technical in thought than a typical private letter. When compared to other ancient letters outside of the New Testament, they are actually significantly longer. This, however, is not surprising when you consider how much the apostles needed to accomplish as shepherds caring for the churches while they themselves were often away on missionary journeys.

The epistles, for the most part, were written to teach theology and its ethical implications to the Christian community. Because the letters were principally written to instruct the early church, they present fewer difficulties for interpretation than other types of biblical literature. The intent of the letters is clearly stated; and the progression of thought, arguments, and examples is more straightforward than in other types of literature. All of this makes for easier reading for the average Christian who does not have formal training in theology.

THE OCCASION FOR THE LETTER

The New Testament Epistles can be divided into three general classifications of letters: The Pauline Epistles (the letters written by the apostle Paul), the General Epistles (James; 1 and 2 Peter; 1, 2, and 3 John; and Jude), and the Book of Hebrews. Some letters were written to individual churches, such as

Philippians; or to a group of churches in a region, such as the letter to the Galatians; or in the case of Philemon, to an individual. While letters were originally written to a specific group for a specific reason, they were eventually circulated among the entire Christian community.

The specific reason for the letter is called the "occasion for the letter." Understanding the occasion is crucial for its interpretation. The occasion provides the context for the teachings that are presented in the letter and lends insight into the details that may be alluded to in it but that are not specifically addressed.

Let's look at the Book of Galatians as an example. The occasion for the epistle to the Galatians was primarily to counteract the teachings of the Judaizers. They taught that Gentiles had to first become Jews before they could be saved. In addition, they opposed Paul's teaching that salvation was by grace through faith alone and continued to teach a salvation by works. Finally, they challenged Paul's authority and asserted that he was not a legitimate apostle. Knowing the occasion for the letter impacts our understanding of the book.

Paul was not writing this letter to cause the people to ponder his theology; rather, he was writing to combat false teachings that would pull the churches away from following Christ. He was fighting against people who were trying to replace the message of Christ with Judaism that included Christ. Since the Judaizers had attacked Paul's credibility in order to discount his teachings, his vigorous explanation and defense of his *calling to be an apostle* in chapter 1 (1:1, 11–24) is understandable. After the explanation of his calling, he then addressed the main issue—not to exchange the grace of God for a different gospel. In addition, the occasion drives the content of the letter. For example, you find throughout the entire book the stance that salvation comes through faith, not through the law. Chapter 5:6 sums up this truth: "For in Christ Jesus neither circumcision nor un-circumcision avails anything, but faith working through love."

ONE SIDE OF THE CONVERSATION

The Epistles were written to address specific issues relating to the recipients. However, a problem arises from that fact that we have only one side of the conversation pertaining to these matters. For example, we are limited in our understanding of the Colossian philosophy that endangered the church (Colossians 2:8); and the identity of those who opposed Paul in the Philippians letter remains uncertain (1:15–17, 27, 28; 3:2, 18, 19). At times, a letter such as 2 Thessalonians, makes reference to previous instructions that

The Epistles were written to address specific issues relating to the recipients.

are not preserved for us today (2 Thessalonians 2:5–7). In instances like these, we can draw from other helps such as the Book of Acts or other epistles for clues. Extrabiblical sources can also offer some insights into issues found in the Epistles. For example, historical information regarding the city of Corinth records that the temple to Aphrodite was located near the city. The temple is said to have employed 1,000 cult prostitutes. And yet the temple structure could not possibly have housed this many people, leading to the understanding that these prostitutes were located throughout the city. Knowing this information helps us understand why 1 Corinthians has so much material regarding sexual immorality (5:1–13; 6:12–20; 7:1–40).

TIMELESS PRINCIPLES

Because the Epistles addressed specific issues in the Christian community, it is important to distinguish what part of the teachings contain timeless or universal principles for Christians and what part of the teachings only applied to the original recipients. Particular instructions in the Epistles are "culture bound" and do not pertain to every generation of Christians. For example, the letter of Philemon is a personal letter from Paul to Philemon regarding a runaway slave named Onesimus. Onesimus had stolen from Philemon and fled to Rome, but Paul had come into contact with the runaway and led him to faith in Christ. Paul was sending him back to Philemon to be reconciled with his former master. The letter is a masterful appeal

Particular instructions in the Epistles are "culture bound" and do not pertain to every generation of Christians.

for Philemon to forgive the runaway slave and accept him back into his household. We must, however, be careful to delineate between culture-bound teachings and universal teachings. These teachings, along with other words of Paul concerning slavery (Ephesians 6:5–9; Colossians 3:22—4:1; 1 Timothy 6:1, 2; Titus 2:9, 10), must remain in the context of the culture of the Roman Empire. Therefore, the occasion for the book does not specifically apply to our day, nor does it give a defense of slavery. Instead, the description of Philemon's life (verses 4–7) provides one of the greatest examples of a godly church member in the New Testament. Further, the manner in which Paul intervenes in gentleness, kindness, and respect to solve this problem between two Christian brothers offers powerful principles for every Christian. Do not automatically discount a passage or instruction as "culture bound," but rather, look to see if there is a universal teaching present.

A TYPICAL FORM

The form of a New Testament letter is quite similar to letters that we would write today; it contains an introduction, a body, and a conclusion. The introduction, or salutation, begins with an identification of the author and the recipients, a greeting, and a prayer. The body of the letter contains the reasons for the letter, the theological instructions, and the practical methods to enable the reader to "live out" the teachings. The conclusion includes a final prayer along with items such as travel plans, recommendations of coworkers, and greetings.

Not all the New Testament Epistles conform strictly to this pattern. Hebrews, for example, does not clearly state the identity of the author, nor does it have a typical conclusion. The Book of James starts like a typical letter, but seems to end with a collection of short statements or sermonic appeals. While some of these letters vary in form, they all contain the marks of an epistle and are valuable for our study.

APPROACHING AN EPISTLE

The first step in understanding an epistle is to read the entire book in one sitting in order to gain the general ideas and flow of the book. This would be a typical response today if you were to receive a letter or e-mail; you would sit down and read it through. You would not read a paragraph a day until you finished the letter several weeks later. This first reading is not meant to find all the nuances of the letter, but rather to gain a basic understanding of the content.

Second, discover the setting and occasion of the letter. You will be able to discover this information from your first reading. The setting provides a context for the letter, adding to the meaning of the text. For example, knowing that Paul was in prison when he wrote the Book of Philippians, a book marked by the joy found in Christ, gives greater depth to Paul's teachings. To find the occasion, ask yourself the question, "Why did the author write the letter?" The purpose may not be clearly stated in the letter, but is usually apparent from the opening content. For example, the Epistle of James does not openly state the purpose of the letter. However, the letter begins with a discussion about trials and concludes with a call to help those who have wandered from the truth. From this you can see that the occasion for the letter was to encourage the Christian community's members who were under the strain of poverty and persecution.

Once you have a general feel for the book and understand the setting and occasion, you can begin to go deeper into the text. You should start with large divisions of the text and work your way to the finer details and smaller sections of the book. A good way to approach this is to outline the chapters, then move to sections within the chapters, then to paragraphs, and finally to groupings of verses. Your common practice may be to slowly work your way through a book verse by verse. This will come in time, but it is well worth the effort to start with the "big picture" of the letter and then move into the finer details of the letter.

> *As you study the Epistles, you will recognize issues in the early church that are quite relevant today.*

As you study the Epistles, you will quickly discover why they have become such a favorite area of study for most Christians. You will recognize issues in the early church that are quite relevant today. Though culture and context change with time, human nature remains the same. So be prepared to have the apostles speak directly to your life individually and corporately as you study.

CHAPTER

18

❦

REVELATION

*"Blessed is he who reads and those who hear the words
of this prophecy, and keep those things which are written in it; for the time is near."*

Revelation 1:3

*J*f you were to ask a group of Christians the question,
"Which book of the New Testament is the most difficult to understand?" a majority of them would
answer, "Revelation." In fact, a quick look through Christian
bookstores reveals numerous books with multiple opinions
concerning Revelation's interpretation. There is often a great
divide between the popular authors and the academic
authors concerning what Revelation means and how it
should be applied in life. In this chapter, we hope to provide
you with some general rules for interpreting Revelation and
for understanding of the various approaches to interpretation.

WHAT SORT OF WRITING IS THIS?

The beginning point for understanding Revelation is to determine its literary classification. Revelation's *type of literature* is not as easily identifiable as that of other New Testament books. Revelation is unique in that it can be placed into three categories of literature: epistolary (letter-type), prophetic, and apocalyptic. The book should not be limited to one single category, but is better understood as a blending of all three genres.

Revelation is first and foremost an epistle as it contains an opening introduction to the seven churches of Asia (1:4). Notice the specific address in Revelation 1:11: "What you see, write in a book and send *it* to the seven churches which are in Asia: to Ephesus, to Smyrna, to Pergamos, to Thyatira, to Sardis, to Philadelphia, and to Laodicea." The identification of Revelation as a letter is further supported by its closing words: "The grace of our Lord Jesus Christ *be* with you all. Amen" (22:21). This is a standard closing to an epistle and is mirrored in every letter of the apostle Paul and in the Book of Hebrews.

While Revelation is a letter to the churches in Asia, the author specifically designates his material as prophecy (1:3; 19:10; 22:7, 18, 19). Therefore, it is not surprising that the closest biblical parallels to Revelation are portions of the Old Testament prophetic books—Isaiah, Jeremiah, and Ezekiel.

The third classification, apocalyptic literature, is taken from the opening words of the text "The Revelation of Jesus Christ." "Apocalypse" is from a Greek word that means *revelation, unveiling, disclosing,* or *revealing.* Apocalyptic literature was common in Palestine between approximately 200 B.C. and A.D. 100. It first emerged during times of great hardship and persecution. Typically, the recipients of this literature were in need of encouragement and hope for the future. They needed to have hope that God would intervene, provide an end to their immediate suffering, and grant them victory over their enemies. Apocalyptic writing is connected to a critical historical situation in which the occasion is illustrated through vivid imagery. The message of the writings was presented through visions carrying a predictive element. This type of literature makes extensive use of symbolism to emphasize conflict between good and evil.

To gain a thorough understanding of Revelation, read it in light of all three types of literature. The text was sent as a circular letter to the churches in Asia who were under persecution. The letter designates itself as prophecy. It would have been appropriate to circulate such a letter to these suffering churches, because the New Testament explains the reason for prophecy this way: "he who prophesies speaks edification and exhortation and comfort to men" (1 Corinthians 14:3). And much of the book is written in the style of apocalyptic literature that was prominent during the time the letter was penned.

APPROACHING REVELATION

There are three different approaches to understanding this last book of the New Testament: the Preterist View, the Futurist View, and the Idealist View.

The Preterist View

The Preterist view sees Revelation as specifically relating to the issues of the early Christian church. It takes the position that the fulfillment of Revelation had already come to pass during the time of the Roman Empire.

The Futurist View

In the Futurist view, apart from the first few chapters of Revelation, the book is believed to be entirely connected to the events concerning the end of the age. This approach does not attribute meaning in the text for the original audience (the seven churches in Asia).

The Idealist View

In the Idealist viewpoint, the Book of Revelation does not depict events from the period of the early church or events that will take place in the future. Rather, it presents ideas, principles, and theological concepts. These timeless truths of God relate to every generation of Christians.

A quick glance at these three approaches may have left you asking yourself, "Where do my beliefs fit into these theories?" If so, you are not alone as this is the general consensus of many people. Each of these approaches has both merit and weaknesses, causing many to adapt a *blended approach* to Revelation. The letter first had meaning and application for the early church, but it also contained a predictive element that applies to the end of the age. Further, the truths presented to the early church contain timeless principles that apply to every generation of Christians.

A BLENDED APPROACH

Remember that when reading the Scripture, you should first ask, "What was the meaning of this text for its original audience?" Too often when interpreting Revelation there is a tendency to think about what the book is saying about the future. If the book is only concerned with the future, then it would have had no meaning for its original audience—the seven churches in Asia. Remember that John wrote in his opening verse that what he was about to say "must shortly take place"; and then he reminded his readers, "The time is near" (1:3). Therefore, the prophecy must have had meaning and fulfillment for the members of the early church.

The people of the early church had believed the gospel and received the hope that Christ would come back to defeat evil and establish His kingdom. In light of the persecution of the church, the Christians were beginning to question whether the claims of Christianity were true. From their perspective, things were not getting better. The letter was sent to a small church that was in the middle of persecution, overwhelmed by their circumstances, and slipping away from the beliefs they had held. They did not know how to relate the claims of Christianity to their current situation. John wrote to let the people know that the Roman Empire did not control the future; only the risen Christ controlled the destiny of the world. Through numerous visions, John made it clear that God alone is in control. The visions were rooted in the setting of the Roman Empire, but they present timeless truths concerning God that apply to every generation. Understanding that the visions were grounded in the setting of the early church helps guard against tendencies to quickly apply the truths of Revelation to modern events, politics, and technology. Always look for the timeless truths concerning God rather than attempting to place a meaning on the text that could never have been imagined fifty years ago, let alone 1,900 years ago.

THE USE OF SYMBOLISM

When reading Revelation, you can quickly become overwhelmed by its extensive use of symbolism. In fact, most of the symbols found in Revelation are quite mysterious. However, John did explain some of his symbolism. For instance, he stated that the seven stars and the seven lampstands are angels and churches (Revelation 1:20). Further, he related the bowls of incense to the prayers of the saints (5:8), and the dragon was portrayed as the Devil (12:9). These examples are rare as most of the symbols throughout the book are left unexplained.

While there is no simple solution for interpreting the symbols, it is important to identify which symbols are to be understood *figuratively* and which ones are to be read *literally*. The best rule is to take an individual approach to each symbol. In order to accurately interpret the symbols, you must become familiar with the historical background and theological significance of the symbols. At this point, a good commentary will prove to be helpful. If you are only going to buy one or two books on Revelation, be careful to buy ones that are described as *commentaries*. If possible, buy a commentary that is part of a set of commentaries where the authors have been chosen because of their expertise in New Testament studies. The reason that we suggest buying a commentary from a set that is written by multiple authors is that the publisher will always try to enlist the most qualified person to write each individual book. The date a commentary has been published is also an important consideration in your purchase, since older commentaries do not have the benefit of the most recent discoveries from archaeology, updated textual studies, and current theories.

There are also instances where the symbols used have direct ties to the Old Testament. Revelation makes extensive use of the Old Testament. At times, these references are very clear while at other times they can be vague. Utilizing a cross-reference system will enhance your understanding of the symbols found in Revelation.

Many Bibles contain a cross-reference system that will indicate when a passage or symbol can be linked to an Old Testament passage. For example, the words "He who overcomes, I will make him a pillar in the temple of My God" (3:12) can be viewed in light of 1 Kings 7, which describes the pillars of the temple. The description of John eating the scroll that "was as sweet as honey in my mouth. But when I had eaten it, my stomach became bitter" (10:9) has obvious associations to the scroll eaten by Ezekiel in chapter 3 of his book. The plagues described in chapter 15 have an evident relationship to the plagues described in Exodus 15. When you find an allusion to an Old Testament event, location, person, or teaching, be careful to read the Old Testament reference. Looking back to the passage being alluded to can provide valuable insights. However, do not automatically assume that the Revelation passage means exactly the same thing as the Old Testament passage. Rather, recognize that Revelation will have a *New Testament perspective* and may further develop or add to the Old Testament passage to teach a specific truth.

When you find an allusion to an Old Testament event, location, person, or teaching, be careful to read the Old Testament reference.

THE USE OF NUMBERS

Numbers are used in Revelation in a repetitive manner indicating that they have more significance than their literal numerical meaning. Many of its numbers are used symbolically in other parts of the Bible. Therefore, when you encounter a number that appears to have a symbolic meaning, look to other examples of this number for your interpretation. For example: the number seven is used for the group of churches receiving the book (1:4); the seals on the scroll (5:1); the trumpet judgments (8:2); and the bowl judgments (16:1). Seven is used throughout the Scriptures (see, for examples, Genesis 41:27; Leviticus 26:18; Joshua 6:4; Psalm 119:164;

Matthew 18:21) and is understood to signify "completeness." Numbers can also be multiplied to indicate significance. Do not assume that the numbers found in Revelation are to be taken literally. Look to see if a number has a particular meaning attached to it in other parts of the Bible or if a number is a multiple of a significant digit to determine if it should be interpreted figuratively or literally.

IMPORTANT THEMES

In a brief overview such as this, it is impossible to address all of the interpretation issues of Revelation. One can find hope from John's words in 22:10: "And he said to me, 'Do not seal the words of the prophecy of this book, for the time is at hand.'" We can trust that as we seek honestly to interpret Revelation, the Holy Spirit will be faithful to open our understanding and apply the words of this book to our hearts in practical ways. No matter how difficult its interpretation may seem, God did not intend for Revelation to remain a mystery to His people. While you may not be able to understand every symbol or vision, you will be able to draw from the general teachings and will grow in your relationship to God.

Revelation provides truths concerning the sovereignty of God that are unparalleled in any other book of the New Testament. The picture of Christ and the worship that is due Him will bring Christians into a deeper understanding of the "Lamb that was slain," who is worthy of our worship. There is much to be learned concerning the reality of evil in this world and the spiritual battle that involves every believer.

Remember, Christ provided this revelation to be a source of encouragement to His people and to assure His children of His ultimate victory over evil. This book provides hope for the discouraged, confirms God's resolve to defeat and judge evil, and promises great rewards for every person who endures—that his or her name is indeed written in the Lamb's Book of Life.

19

❦

EXEGESIS: FURTHER STUDY—PART 1

Now a certain Jew named Apollos, born at Alexandria, an eloquent man and mighty in the Scriptures, came to Ephesus. This man had been instructed in the way of the Lord; and being fervent in spirit, he spoke and taught accurately the things of the Lord.

Acts 18:24, 25

*E*veryone needs to be able to read the Bible with understanding. Some, however, desire to go beyond simple understanding to further in-depth study. What you emphasize depends on your purpose for study. The following is a list of different types of study you can bring to the Bible.

BIOGRAPHICAL STUDY

Beyond just knowing the identity of the characters in the Bible as you read, you may want to engage in a comprehensive *biographical study*. When asking the question, "Who is this character?" you may discover some fascinating information that is not available in the immediate context of your text. This is a wonderful exercise that will make the stories in the Bible much more enjoyable to read. When you understand people, whether they are the author or a character in the book, you will discover a realism that you never saw before.

The people in the Bible were real! They lived in real places, had real families, and faced real problems just like you do. They become examples that inspire you or examples to warn you. Their encounters with God can give insight into a relationship that pleases Him. When referring to people in the Old Testament, the apostle Paul said that "with most of them God was not well pleased, for *their bodies* were scattered in the wilderness. Now these things became our examples, to the intent that we should not lust after evil things as they also lusted. And do not become idolaters as *were* some of them" (1 Corinthians 10:5–7).

To begin your study of Bible personalities, consider what their names mean. Their names often reflect their character

The people in the Bible were real! They lived in real places, had real families, and faced real problems just like you do.

and give insight into the way they might be expected to act. There are many specialized books in this field, but even a general Bible dictionary will likely give you this information. Compare several different tools to get a better understanding of a name. Consider the following names: "Esau" means "Hairy"; "Isaac" means "Laughing One"; "David" means "Beloved"; "Hosea" means "Salvation"; "Timothy" means "Honoring God"; and "Jesus" means "Yahweh Is Salvation."

Next, look at all the passages that refer to the person you are studying. Use a concordance to find all the references and construct a list of where the person is found in the Bible. As you read, make several lists to organize the information:

1) Gather basic biographical information about when and where the person was born, who his or her parents were, any other significant relatives, occupation, and so on.

2) Outline the person's life. Try and trace a chronological progression of the person's actions, including geographical movement. This will often give insights into the personal growth of an individual throughout his or her life.

3) Identify character traits. List both the positive traits to be followed and the negative traits to be avoided. In one clear statement, describe the character of the person.

4) Summarize the person's relationship to God. You may observe a great change within a person. If you are studying a significant character, you may discover that the growing relationship parallels a growing character. For example, the older, more mature Peter was not the same man Jesus pulled off the boat to be His disciple.

All the information gathered about an individual is for the purpose of application. What have you learned about the person as he or she related to God? What lessons can you apply to your own life? What have you learned about the nature of God and His relationship with you? Apply what you have learned to all four areas of your life: your relationship to God; your own life; your relationship to other people; and your involvement in the church.

WORD STUDIES

We mentioned earlier the need for word studies. As you study a particular scripture, the question you need to ask is this: "What are the significant words, and what do they mean in this context?" In your study of words, you may want to do an etymological study, which is tracing the history of a word. While this exercise can be helpful, there are some cautions to such a study. 1) Often, the original meanings are conjectural. We make our best guess, but there may still be some ambiguity. 2) The original meanings of a word and its use today may be very different. For example, the English word "nice" comes from *nescius*, which means "ignorant." 3) Beware of reading English words back into Greek or Hebrew words. For example, the English word "dynamite" is derived from the Greek word *dunamis*, which means "power." The contemporary word "dynamite" is not the best understanding of the original word. 4) Meaning is also determined by usage in context.

Most word studies begin with a contemporary word and go back to the original language, in the hope of discovering what the word meant at the time it was written. That means we are seeking the original meaning of the author who used the word in Scripture. Thus, etymology may not help us, since the word may have changed meaning from the time the author used it. Start by trusting your English translation and look up the word in an English dictionary. Consider the synonyms and antonyms as a way to better grasp the concept. If you have any ability with the original languages, you can look up a word in a Greek or Hebrew lexicon. You don't have to be an expert!

Next, discover the biblical use of the word. There are several tools you can use for this step. First, a good study Bible may have a definition in its footnotes or highlighted in the text. Second, an exhaustive concordance will help you find all the places it is used in the Bible. Move on to a Bible dictionary to help you understand the word. You will quickly discover that reading the word in different contexts will bring new light to its fuller meaning.

The last step in a word study is to write a definition in your own words. It is fine to memorize what others have said, but to give a definition that comes from your own thoughts indicates you fully grasp its meaning. As in all studies, you must then apply what you have learned to all four areas of your life: your relationship to God; your own life; your relationship to other people; and your involvement in the church.

SYNTHETIC STUDIES

The question of a synthetic study of a book is this: "What is the purpose of this book, and how do particular passages fit into the bigger picture?" For this type of study, you need to get an overview of the entire book and to grasp how each part fits together. Synthetic study attempts to get the big picture and not get lost in the details. The benefits of such a study are that you keep from going off on tangents or building a whole doctrine around a single verse.

The question of a synthetic study of a book is this: "What is the purpose of this book, and how do particular passages fit into the bigger picture?"

The first step is to read through the entire book, preferably in one sitting. Long books will take a few hours, but it is still worth the effort to get the flow of a book. As you read, ignore the chapter numbers and the individual verses. The numbers were not in the original text anyway, but were added later for our benefit. Don't take time to make notes on this first read; just keep the flow and get through the book. Also, read the book independently. That is, don't consult a commentary or other reference books in this initial reading, but trust the Holy Spirit to guide your thinking.

Once you have read the book through completely, read it again. This time, keep a notepad handy, and write down your thoughts as you go. Look for things that will help you understand the book: the author, the recipients, the style of writing, the issues addressed, the emotional tone of the book, the arrangement of material, and so on. Especially look for statements that give the author's purpose. For example, John states his purpose for writing the epistle of 1 John: "These things I have written to you who believe in the name of the Son of God, that you may know that you have eternal life, and that you may continue to believe in the name of the Son of God" (1 John 5:13). Luke also used the first four verses of his Gospel to give his purpose in writing. For this second reading, it may be helpful to use a different translation than you chose for your first read. In fact, multiple translations will broaden your understanding if you have time to read a book several times.

Once you can see the purpose, content, and structure of the book, it is time to examine its sections. Look at how the author arranged his thoughts and identify the theme of each group of paragraphs. Some Bibles have already added a heading or title to these groupings, but attempt it for yourself. Look for connections between paragraphs and see if the author is moving chronologically, building one thought upon another, or just discussing random issues. A key indicator is the transition word. If you see the word "therefore," you know that what comes next is a result of what came before it.

Finally, look at the major sections of the book. These will take the form of chapters or larger sections of material that may even span more than one chapter. For example, Jesus' Sermon on the Mount extends through chapters 5—7 of Matthew. Try and give a title for these major sections and see the overall flow of the book. By the time you finish this exercise, you should have a good grasp of the particular book you are studying. In turn, the smaller passages within the book will have greater meaning. But don't end your study without applying what you have learned. Consider how the truths learned impact your relationship to God; your own life; your relationship to other people; and your involvement in the church.

20

꩜

EXEGESIS: FURTHER STUDY—PART 2

When wisdom enters your heart, and knowledge is pleasant to your soul, discretion will preserve you; understanding will keep you.

Proverbs 2:10, 11

ANALYTICAL STUDIES

Whereas a synthetic study looks at the big picture of an entire book, an analytical study will focus on the details of a passage within a book. It is best to begin with a synthetic study, but there is often need to analyze a particular passage with greater scrutiny. The question is: "What does *this* passage mean?" This narrowed focus leads to close observation of the details. This method, therefore, is concerned with a verse or small group of verses within the text.

The first step after identifying a passage for analysis is to read it several times in several different translations. This may seem very simple, but your familiarity with the passage and its variant readings is invaluable to understanding the content. You will know that you have grasped the passage if you can paraphrase it in your own words and remain true to its meaning. When the passage becomes *yours*, it will come alive with meaning.

Next, begin asking questions of the passage. Who said it? To whom was it given? Why was it said? And what difference does it

An analytical study will focus on the details of a passage within a book.

make? Use every angle to question the passage, considering many different perspectives. As you review the passage, observe the words more carefully. Are the verbs forceful or commanding? Is the tone gentle or stern? Are certain phrases or themes repeated? Do connecting words tie this passage to what precedes it? You will find that the more you examine verses with this type of questioning, the more questions you will come up with on your own. You will naturally start to see things jump out at you that you would have otherwise missed.

Let's quickly look 1 John 4:20, 21 and make some observations: "If someone says, 'I love God,' and hates his brother, he is a liar; for he who does not love his brother whom he has seen, how can he love God whom he has not seen? And this commandment we have from Him: that he who loves God *must* love his brother also."

- Notice the repetition of words in these two short sentences: "love" (5 times); "God" (3 times); and "brother" (3 times).

- Notice the connection to the larger passage: "love" is used 27 times in chapter 4.

- Notice the strong language: "hate," "liar," "commandment," and "must."

- Notice the rhetorical question: "How can he love God whom he has not seen?"

- Notice the comparison: "love his brother" compared to "love God."

- Notice the word "if." This indicates a condition required.

- Ask, "Who is talking?" The apostle John. He was known as "the disciple whom Jesus loved" (John 21:20).

- Ask, "To whom is this spoken?" Those who claim to be believers in Jesus Christ.

- Ask, "Why is this spoken?" Some who said they loved God obviously were not treating their fellow Christians with the same love.

- Ask, "What difference does it make?" If you don't love your brother, you are a liar and do not have a love relationship with God.

There are many more questions you could ask and many more observations you could make, but you get the idea. A proper analysis of these two verses would also spend more time in the context, which will obviously give much more insight into this particular passage.

Once you have gained as much insight into these verses as you can, compare them with similar verses in other parts of the Bible. Some resources to help in the search include a concordance, a topical Bible, a cross-reference tool, and a commentary on that passage. You will be looking for similar words, similar events, or similar characters. We will say it again: "The Bible is the best commentary on the Bible." Comparing your passage with similar passages will provide great insight and will clarify issues that may be a little vague when the verses stand alone.

Last, you want to summarize your findings and apply them to your life. God is always speaking to your situation as you read the Scriptures, so allow the Holy Spirit to take the truths and make them real. Use the tools you learned about earlier as you make the application. Is this descriptive or prescriptive? Is this a specific practice to be repeated or a principle to be followed and so on? Once you clearly understand what the passage means, ask the Holy Spirit to make the application in the four areas of concern: your relationship to God; your own life; your relationship to other people; and your involvement in the church.

BIBLICAL BACKGROUND STUDIES

As you study the Bible, the question inevitably arises, "How does the Bible itself fit into the scheme of history?" It is good to remember that Israel was not the only nation in the world, that David was not the only king in the world, that the New Testament language of Greek was from a foreign land, that religious festivals were steeped in tradition, that the terrain of Israel is much different from what most of us have ever known, and that most of the Bible takes place in a territory of land approximately 150 miles long by 90 miles wide. In other words, the Bible was not written in a vacuum; there is a context.

To study the background to the Bible can take you on a journey that extends even beyond the biblical text. Surrounding nations also have historical records that shed light on their relationship to Israel. The knowledge of ancient Egypt gives perspective to the Exodus and the struggle to free God's people. The advancing technology and innovations in warfare also enlighten our understanding of the world in which the Bible was written.

There are four main areas of background study: historical, cultural, sociological, and geographical.

There are four main areas of background study: historical, cultural, sociological, and geographical. The tools necessary for such a study include a Bible atlas, Bible encyclopedias, a Bible handbook, general Old and New Testament surveys, commentaries, a concordance, and other specific reference books on the history of Israel. There is not adequate space in this introduction to fully develop this type of Bible study, so let's quickly look at a passage and take note of relevant background information.

Consider the story found in John 4:3–42. Take time to read the whole passage, but for our purposes, it begins as follows: "He left Judea and departed again to Galilee. But He needed to go through Samaria. So He came to a city of Samaria which is called Sychar, near the plot of ground that Jacob gave to his son Joseph. Now Jacob's well was there. Jesus therefore, being wearied from *His* journey, sat thus by the well. It was about the sixth hour. A woman of Samaria came to draw water. Jesus said to her, 'Give me a drink.'"

To the one who is not familiar with information gained through biblical background studies this appears to be a simple story. Let's look from a *historical* perspective. Plainly stated, the Jews hated the Samaritans. Why? Samaria had been the capital of the northern kingdom when it was captured by the Assyrians in 722 B.C. Many of the leading citizens had been deported and replaced with idol-worshiping foreigners (2 Kings 17:24–31). They eventually intermarried and adopted a form of Judaism—a form unacceptable to pious Jews. The rivalry between the Jews and these "half-breeds" often became spiteful. When the Samaritans offered to help rebuild the temple, their help was refused (Ezra 4:2, 3). When they built their own temple on Mount Gerizim, the Jews burned it down. You could say that the Jews and Samaritans had a history!

Let's now see the *cultural* elements to this story. This takes into account an understanding of religions, science, music, art, literature, and philosophy. The element that appears relevant here is religion. We already mentioned that foreign gods were brought into this area by the Assyrians. This resulted in a strong religious clash between the Samaritans and the Jews. So much so, that a pious Jew would not travel through the area. Jesus, however, chose to go against the grain and enter into a region considered "unclean."

The next piece of helpful background information is *geographical*. We mentioned that Jews did not travel through Samaria because of a religious dispute. But we didn't mention that the alternate route was significantly farther. That may not mean much today with our various modes of efficient transportation, but people back then had to walk! They would take a route that crossed over the Jordan River to the east into Perea and Decapolis (the ten cities) and then back across the Jordan River again to the west. Jesus actually took the most direct route from Judea to Galilee.

There are also *sociological* issues in this story. According to the text, Jesus arrived at "Jacob's well" at the "sixth hour," which was noon. It was not common for a woman to be at a public place at that time of day, for they normally would go at sunset. This woman, however, was immoral and was most likely shunned by the other women. She had been married five times and was currently living with another man. Coming at noon may have been her way of avoiding the other women who looked down their noses at her. But even more significant is the fact that women were not to interact with men. In fact, most men would not even talk to their own wife in public. The fact that Jesus spoke with her was significant, knowing the sociological norm of the day. You can tell how dramatic this was even within the passage; for when the disciples saw Him conversing with the woman, they were alarmed (John 4:27).

Can you see how background knowledge brings many elements of Scripture to life? The more you understand, the more powerful the stories become. Make use of available tools to gain such insight; and once again, make the contemporary application: in your relationship to God; your own life; your relationship to other people; and your involvement in the church.

DOCTRINAL STUDIES

One last type of Bible study to consider is doctrinal (focusing on principles of belief). The question is this: "How does this text fit in a doctrinal system?"

There are three basic systems for organizing biblical truth. First is through Biblical Theology, which organizes theological teachings by the portions of the Bible in which they occur rather than by topic. For example, the Pentateuch, Wisdom Literature, the Prophets, and the Synoptics are some of the major Bible portions. A second method for organizing biblical truth is through Historical Theology. Theological teachings are organized through chronological development from

One last type of Bible study to consider is doctrinal (focusing on principles of belief).

biblical times to the present. Historical Theology takes into account the theological decisions of church councils, creeds and confessions of faith, and the writings of individual theologians. A third method of organizing biblical truth, called Systematic Theology, is a topical organization of theological teachings. This method utilizes the results of Biblical and Historical

Theology, but seeks to express teachings in a contemporary form and to relate them to issues of practical Christian concern. A basic outline of Systematic Theology would include the following categories: 1) Revelation and Authority; 2) God's Nature and Attributes; 3) Creation; 4) Humanity; 5) Sin; 6) Christ's Person and Work; 7) Salvation; 8) Holy Spirit's Person and Work; 9) The Church; and 10) Eschatology.

When approaching theological studies, an attitude of humility is required. Humility comes from the knowledge that revelation is only partial and there are some things we don't need to know. It also comes from the fact that we are finite. Even if revelation were full, we could not fully comprehend it. Finally, humility recognizes the fact that we are fallen. Sin has warped our understanding (Romans 3), and our sinful nature tends to twist and turn and rationalize until the Scripture means what we want it to mean. As a result, we need an open mind and a willingness to learn.

That being said, follow three important guidelines in developing a systematic theology. First, base doctrine on a sound exegesis of the text, that is, make sure you understand what the Bible is saying through proper principles of interpretation. Second, base doctrine on the entire Bible. Organize the information as you consider parallel passages and contrasting ideas. But as you gather the information, follow these important rules:

1. The clear passage is to be preferred above the obscure.
2. Greater weight is to be given to teaching often repeated.
3. Direct, literal teaching should be given preference.
4. Later revelation takes precedence over earlier revelation in building doctrine.

The last guideline is to base doctrine solely on the Bible. Don't build on inference; don't build on tradition; and don't build on other extrabiblical sources. Doctrine should only reflect Bible emphases.

There are many good theology books to keep as reference tools. Don't be afraid of them, for they can help you put a particular passage into the larger discussion of the topic. Consider purchasing several different theology books for your library and keep them handy. As you study the great doctrines of the Bible, apply them to your relationship to God; your own life; your relationship to other people; and your involvement in the church.

SECTION

THREE

CHANGED BY GOD
THROUGH HIS WORD:

THE TRANSFORMATION

CHAPTER

21

☙

OBEDIENCE

Jesus answered and said to him, "If anyone loves Me, he will keep My word; and My Father will love him, and We will come to him and make Our home with him."

John 14:23

*I*f you want to experience God in your life, you must deal with the word "obedience." Without obedience, you cannot know God as He intended. You may come to know Him as Judge, but not as Savior and Friend. You can fill your head full of biblical knowledge and believe it with all your heart; but without obedience, it means nothing. We have already discussed obedience in a limited fashion, but it needs to be anchored into your thinking as we bring this book to a close. Obedience is the key to experiencing God.

A TRUST RELATIONSHIP

When God speaks, the subject is not up for discussion. His commands are not given so that you can pick and choose which ones you want to obey. He doesn't give suggestions! He is God, and we are not; He is the Master, and we are the servants. He expects that we will obey everything He says if we are truly His people. An important question for you to consider is this: "Do you trust God?" You know what the right answer is, but is it true of your life? Do you trust God with every detail of your life? If you don't trust Him, you will not obey Him. The key to trusting God, however, is knowing God; for the more you know Him, the more you will trust Him.

The more you know [God], the more you will trust Him.

Consider Jesus' statement in Matthew 7:21–23: "Not everyone who says to Me, 'Lord, Lord,' shall enter the kingdom of heaven, but he who does the will of My Father in heaven. Many will say to Me in that day, 'Lord, Lord, have we not prophesied in Your name, cast out demons in Your name, and done many wonders in Your name?' And I will declare to them, 'I never knew you; depart from Me, you who practice lawlessness!'" In this passage, Jesus clearly states that obedience to the Father's will is paramount; it is the evidence of salvation. And no matter what we say, obedience is the indication that we know God. It doesn't matter if you say, "I know the Lord." It only matters if the Lords says, "I know you."

Let us illustrate with a true story. Our family has been blessed with many opportunities to meet with influential people. On one occasion, some of us met the president of the United States at a dinner and had our picture taken with him. It is a great picture with smiles all around. So let me ask the question: "Do I know the president?" I know his name, a lot of personal facts about him, voted for him, and even have a great picture with him! But none of those things mean that I *truly* know him. Let me turn that question to ask: "Does the president know me?" No, I was just one face among many. And if I tried to run up to him, he would quickly summon the Secret Service to haul me away and put me in custody. I know *about* the president and have even been around him, but I don't know him. Really getting to know someone takes time and involves relationship.

On the Judgment Day, it does not matter if we can say, "I know Christ" but if Christ can say, "I know you." He may very well say, "Depart from Me; I never knew you." And if we reply, "But, Lord, I know You! I went to church, and I saw You! I read the Bible and learned all about You!" He may answer, "Gaining eternal life depends not on whether you know Me, but on whether I know you. And if I knew you, then I would have taken up residence in your life and you would be filled with all the fullness of God. But isn't it obvious that I never took up residence in your life? The old life is still there. When I spoke, you never answered. When I required your service, you refused. When I called you to follow Me, you turned the other way. You may call Me Lord, but you never obeyed anything I said to you."

Obedience is the fruit of a trust relationship; it is evidence of salvation. If you know Christ and He knows you, it will be obvious by your obedient lifestyle. If He is in you, *His life* will make a radical difference in *your life* (2 Corinthians 5:17). The apostle Paul urges us, "Examine yourselves *as to* whether you are in the faith. Test yourselves. Do you not know yourselves, that Jesus Christ is in you?—unless indeed you are disqualified?" (2 Corinthians 13:5).

You cannot trust God if you do not know God. That is why Bible study is so critical to the Christian life; for the more you know Him, the easier it is to trust Him. And every step of obedience opens up new opportunities to know Him.

AN EXPRESSION OF LOVE

We tend to express obedience in terms of fulfilling a duty, a disciplined life, or even conquering a task. Jesus, however, always keeps obedience in the context of love. He said, "If anyone loves Me, he will keep My word" (John 14:23). No matter what you say about your love for God, obedience is the only measurement that God is using. As far as He is concerned, this is His estimation of your relationship: no obedience = no love; absolute obedience = absolute love.

The apostle Paul understood the relationship. He made a profound statement in 2 Corinthians 5:14, 15: "For the love of Christ compels us, because we judge thus: that if One died for all, then all died; and He died for all, that those who live should live no longer for themselves, but for Him who died for them and rose again." Love was the motivation of Paul's life. It was the compelling force that produced obedience to Christ. That is why the "love relationship" to Christ ought to be the focus of our life. Not obedience to the commands of God, but love for the Son of God. Obedience is simply a by-product of the relationship.

Remember, the Bible is your guide to a deeper relationship with God, so don't be discouraged if reading it sometimes causes you to see inadequacies in your life. The Bible helps you see yourself as God sees you; and once you know what is on His heart , you can release your life to Him, and He will move you from where you are to where He wants you to be.

AN OPPORTUNITY TO EXPERIENCE GOD

You have seen how obedience flows from a love relationship. But what you also need to know is that experiencing God in your life comes after you obey. When you obey Him, you are partnering with Him as He works in our world today. It will surprise you what He will accomplish through your life if you will just respond and obey. But if you do not obey, you will miss out on some of the most exciting things that He had in store for you.

Jesus said, "If anyone loves Me, he will keep My word" (John 14:23). That statement is an absolute; it is a spiritual reality. Obedience does not produce love; love produces obedience. It is always in that order. But the result of your love for God is not just obedience; you also experience a deepening relationship. This verse continues with a powerful promise from the Lord. To those who love and obey His word, "My Father will love him, and We will come to him and make Our home with him." Wow, *that* is relationship! God the Father and God the Son will abide within. Jesus would later include God the Spirit (John 16:7), and the entire Trinity would take up residence in those who love and obey. It always comes back to the love relationship.

Let's return to the topic of Bible study and obedience. If you study the Bible in the hope that God will direct you, enlighten you, and even speak to your heart, you must have a heart of ready obedience. Before you ever hear Him, you must answer "Yes." And the reason you must have a heart of ready obedience is that He cannot teach you the greater things of the kingdom until He has taught you the basics: Lordship. It is a waste of time for the Lord to show you the path He wants you to take if you have not yet decided to follow Him, if you don't fully trust Him, and if you don't really love Him.

If you want to go deeper into God's Word, you must follow Him every step of the way.

So what is your answer? If there is a hesitation, don't expect to hear Him; you have not yet settled the fact that He is Lord. Don't expect to get very far in your understanding of God's Word, for He can't take you further than you are prepared to go. Did not Jesus say to His disciples, "I still have many things to say to you, but you cannot bear *them* now" (John 16:12)? They could not handle greater truths until they had mastered the basic truths. There is a foundation that must be laid before the Lord can build upon it. This is why obedience to the last thing God said is so important; this is why obedience is necessary in Bible study. If you want to go deeper into God's Word, you must follow Him *every* step of the way.

22

☙

NOT FOR YOU ALONE

One generation shall praise Your works to another, and shall declare Your mighty acts.

Psalm 145:4

MUTUAL INTERDEPENDENCE

They are watching you; they are listening to you; they are the next generation's members who need to know what you have learned from the Lord. If you have not already understood this truth, listen carefully: When God speaks to you through His Word, it is not for your benefit alone. If you are a Christian, your life is vitally connected to the lives of other believers. When you are born again, you are born into the family of God. God has no orphans; He expects that you will find your place within the family. The apostle Paul demonstrated this connection by using the illustration of a body. "So we, *being many*, are one body in Christ, and individually members of one another" (Romans 12:5). He also said, "The manifestation of the Spirit is given to each one for the profit *of all*" (1 Corinthians 12:7). When God works in your life through His Word, it is for the benefit of the whole body; His work in your life is so that the entire body is built up and encouraged.

Too often people live with such a self-centered view of the world, and even more tragically, of their walk with God. This is not about you, but about what God is doing in you. And He desires to work *in* you so that He can work *through* you in order to bless others in your life. Consider Ephesians 4:11–16 in terms of your love relationship with God within the body of Christ:

And He Himself gave some *to be* apostles, some prophets, some evangelists, and some pastors and teachers, for the equipping of the saints for the work of ministry, for the edifying of the body of Christ, till we all come to the unity of the faith and of the knowledge of the Son of God, to a perfect man, to the measure of the stature of the fullness of Christ; that we should no longer be children, tossed to and fro and carried about with every wind of doctrine, by the trickery of men, in the cunning craftiness of deceitful plotting, but, speaking the truth in love, may grow up in all things into Him who is the head—Christ—from whom the whole body, joined and knit together by what every joint supplies, according to the effective working by which every part does its share, causes growth of the body for the edifying of itself in love.

This entire passage is a powerful statement of our interdependence upon one another in the body of Christ. Do you see how intimately we are related? how precisely God has placed us in the body and equipped us for the purpose of building up one another? God does not want us to be "tossed to and fro and carried about with every wind of doctrine," but to be mature in Christ. That is to happen as we challenge one another and walk together in the church.

As God teaches you through the Scriptures, you must allow His Word to impact the rest of the body; that is how He will build up the entire body. Some are not interested in joining a Bible study or a Sunday school class because they feel as though they already know the material. They must not realize that this is not about them alone. We must put aside a self-centered view of our faith and "share what we know." We can go to a Bible study for what we can contribute as much as for what we can receive. But rest assured, in that environment, we all receive blessings from the Lord—each one using his or her personal walk with God to build another's walk with God.

PRACTICAL SUGGESTIONS

Personal Bible study and prayer are very important to the believer, but so is corporate Bible study and prayer. There are many ways to study the Bible within the context of the body of Christ, each one with a different strategy or focus. We have already mentioned several ways to study Scripture in chapters 19 and 20. These include the study of characters, books of the Bible, biblical words, specific passages, background information, and doctrines. But consider the following ideas when it comes to building up the body through group Bible study.

Teaching Children

One of the best investments you can make is to allow God to shape a child through your life. Proverbs 22:6 says, "Train up a child in the way he should go, and when he is old he will not depart from it." Time invested in teaching God's Word to a child may be the most significant time you spend. D. L. Moody, a famous evangelist, was once asked, "How many converts did you have last night?" He answered, "Two and one-half." The man inquired, "You mean two adults and a child?" Moody explained, "No. Two children and one adult." A child converted is an entire life converted.

One of the best investments you can make is to allow God to shape a child through your life.

Moody was right. Adults converted have already used up half of a lifetime on personal pursuits. We must reach out to children and help them to know God. There is no better way than simple Bible studies.

Ask the Lord if He wants you to get involved in teaching children. You can do it through regular Sunday school, midweek children's programs, or occasional events like Vacation Bible School in the summer. Keep the lessons short and simple with lots of illustrations. But do not underestimate children's ability to comprehend spiritual truth. Their simple faith is their greatest advantage. Jesus said, "Assuredly, I say to you, unless you are converted and become as little children, you will by no means enter the kingdom of heaven" (Matthew 18:3). Why? Because children naturally trust God and receive the gospel with childlike faith.

Continuous Bible Study

The best way for you to learn the Bible is to study it consistently. That sounds simple enough, but many do not take it seriously. Just get involved in a study, whether at church on Sunday morning or in a home during the week. The place and time don't matter nearly as much as the desire to be in God's Word. If you can study with other people, you will gain insights from them and you can offer insights yourself. The interaction is powerful, as the Holy Spirit teaches the group together. You may be called upon to be the facilitator, or you may be one of the participants. Either way, you have something to contribute.

Beware of just studying books *about* the Bible and not the Bible itself. Lesson guides and other teaching helps are fine as supplements, but they should never replace God's Word as your primary focus. It is also important that you cover the entire Bible over time. As important as the Gospels are to life, don't get stuck there; dig into both the Old and New Testaments. Your awareness of the entire Bible will greatly enhance your study of particular passages. Don't rush through the Scripture because you are trying to "get through" the lesson book. Take as much time as necessary to allow the Holy Spirit to say what needs to be said. And never end a study without helping one another apply it to real life.

Topical Bible Study

Topical Bible study helps you to understand life issues and what the Bible has to say about those issues. This approach will not take a book of the Bible and study through it from beginning to end, but will choose passages throughout the entire Bible that address the particular topic. Some popular topical studies are marriage, parenting, finances, prayer, leadership, dealing with depression, and experiencing God.

Topical Bible study helps you to understand life issues and what the Bible has to say about those issues.

These studies are very attractive, for they allow people to address specific personal needs. If you have an area of weakness or a special interest, you can easily address it with a topical study. The caution, however, is not to be so focused that you miss the big picture. Always keep your study in context, and don't just look for things that support your point of view. A balanced Christian life seeks the whole counsel of God and not just points with which one is comfortable.

There are two ways to do such a study: First, you can use a concordance and look up all the verses where the Bible deals with a particular issue. It is a wonderful experience to chase down scriptures and follow the leading of the Holy Spirit through the Word. Second, these studies also tend to lean on books men and women have written about the Bible. So make sure that your study actually deals with Scripture and bases its instruction on the Word of God.

Read-Through

Another approach to studying is to find a group that will commit to just reading through the Bible. Sometimes a pastor or discipleship leader will issue the challenge to an entire church. There are many "read through the Bible in a year" guides available. This technique is considered surface reading and by its very nature cannot go very deep. But that is okay. People need to be familiar with the whole Bible, and a cursory reading can be very beneficial toward this end. Reading through the Bible opens your eyes to parts of the Bible you may never have read before. A read-through of the Bible keeps you aware of the big picture. This is not only a good discipline, but you would be surprised at the way God speaks to you from some "out-of-the-way" passages.

GLOSSARY OF TERMS

GLOSSARY OF TERMS

❧

This list contains terms related to the field of biblical interpretation that were used in this book, as well a few that were not. Nevertheless, it will help you as a quick reference in your further study of the topic.

Allegory — The assumption that the true meaning of the text lies beneath the literal meaning. It ignores the historical significance and interprets without reference to history.

Anthropomorphism — Taking a human characteristic or feature and attributing it to God.

Apocalyptic Literature — Writing that uses symbols or visions regarding the end of the world to express encouragement to God's people who are under persecution.

Canonicity — Books allowed in the Bible. The differentiation of books with divine inspiration from those that are purely works of human origin.

Connotation — An implied emotional meaning of a word apart from its formal meaning.

Cultural Gap — Recognizing the cultural differences between the world in which the Bible was written and the contemporary world (customs, religious belief, science, music, art, and so on).

Denotation — The specific meaning of a word in a dictionary.

Descriptive Narrative — An observation of what happened in history with no obligation to reproduce it.

Dynamic Inspiration — A theory that believes the Holy Spirit worked upon the writers of scripture to make the Bible trustworthy, but not without error in some areas.

Etymology — Tracing the history and origin of a word.

Exegesis — It means "out of (ex) text" and seeks to determine what the biblical writer originally meant.

Figurative Language — A literary device using words with a meaning other than their common or literal sense. It is intended to produce a vivid word picture.

General Revelation — God's self-disclosure in a general way to all people at all times in all places. God reveals Himself through nature, history, and makeup of human nature (conscience).

Hermeneutics — The science and art of biblical interpretation.

Historical Criticism — The study and evaluation of historical evidence to discover information such as the author, dates, historical circumstances, and authenticity of content.

Historical Gap — Recognizing the historical distance between the world in which the Bible was written and the contemporary world (for example, national influences, life context, and economic concerns).

Homiletics — The use of biblical materials in the process of preaching.

Hyperbole — A deliberate exaggeration for the sake of effect.

Illumination — The divine quickening of the human mind, allowing it to understand truth that has been revealed and communicated.

Inspiration — The influence of the Holy Spirit upon the minds of men, which rendered them agents of God for the infallible communication of divine revelation.

Linguistic Gap — Recognizing the linguistic differences between languages used in writing the Bible and that of contemporary languages (Greek, Hebrew, Aramaic, and variant styles of writing).

Literary Criticism — The study of the biblical text as we have it today (grammar, syntax, proper definition of words, and so on).

Meiosis — An intentional understatement.

Metaphor — A direct comparison of two words that does not use *like* or *as*. It is more powerful than a simile.

Noumenological — Written from God's perspective.

Parable — A true-to-life short story designed to teach a truth or to answer a question.

Parallelism — A technique of Hebrew poetry where a thought is expressed on one line, followed by a parallel thought on the next line.

Particular Revelation — God's self-manifestation to particular people at a particular time and place.

Personification — Taking a human characteristic or feature and attributing it to a nonhuman entity.

Phenomenological — Written from a human perspective.

Philosophical Gap — Recognizing philosophical differences between the biblical world view and contemporary thought (Corporate vs. Individualism and so on).

Plenary Inspiration — A doctrine that the Bible is fully inspired. Under the inspiration of the Holy Spirit, the writer used words common to his own vocabulary to describe the revelation given to him.

Prescriptive Narrative — An account of what happened in history for the purpose of instruction or creating a normative pattern to follow.

Progressive Revelation — God's self-manifestation, which is developing and complementary to what had been previously revealed. It is not from untruth to truth, but from lesser to fuller revelation.

Prophetic Literature — Writing that uses real images to give a firm warning to God's people who are in rebellion against Him.

Pseudonym — A fictitious name or a name of a well-known person from the past assumed by a writer who prefers not to use his own name.

Revelation — The act of God whereby He communicates Himself and His will to people.

Simile — A comparison between two words using the words *like* or *as*.

Textual Criticism — The study of the Bible that seeks to discern the original wording of the biblical text.

Verbal Inspiration — A doctrine that the original writings of Scripture were dictated word for word by God. There is no room for the human personality.

Zoomorphism — The representation of God with animal imagery.